TWENTIETH CENTURY VIEWS

The aim of this series is to present the best in contemporary critical opinion on major authors, providing a twentieth century perspective on their changing status in an era of profound revaluation.

Maynard Mack, *Series Editor*
Yale University

DOS PASSOS

A COLLECTION OF CRITICAL ESSAYS

Edited by

Andrew Hook

Prentice-Hall, Inc.  *Englewood Cliffs, N. J.*

A SPECTRUM BOOK

Library of Congress Cataloging in Publication Data

HOOK, ANDREW, comp.
  Dos Passos.

  (Twentieth century views) (A Spectrum Book)
  1. Dos Passos, John, 1896–1970—Criticism and interpretation.
PS3507.0743Z58   813'.5'2   73–21561
ISBN 0–13–218867–8
ISBN 0–13–218859–7 (pbk.)

*For Willard Thorp
In gratitude*

Quotations from *Manhattan Transfer, The Big Money,* and *1919* are used by the kind permission of Elizabeth H. Dos Passos, copyright holder.

10 9 8 7 6 5 4 3 2 1

PRENTICE-HALL INTERNATIONAL, INC. (*London*)
PRENTICE-HALL OF AUSTRALIA PTY. LTD. (*Sydney*)
PRENTICE-HALL OF CANADA LTD. (*Toronto*)
PRENTICE-HALL OF INDIA PRIVATE LIMITED (*New Delhi*)
PRENTICE-HALL OF JAPAN, INC. (*Tokyo*)

Contents

v

Introduction

by Andrew Hook

The problems to be faced in editing a collection of critical essays on John Dos Passos are unusual. The twentieth century has expressed a great many views on a great many writers. And for a long time now no one has been able to complain about any general neglect of American writers of the twentieth or any other century. Faulkner, Hemingway, and Fitzgerald, for example, Dos Passos' contemporaries, have in recent decades been subjected to exhaustive —some would say exhausting—critical attention. Any selection of essays about any one of these is bound to leave a surplus as rich as any butter mountain. With Dos Passos the case is utterly different. The present collection in no way represents a scraping of the critical barrel, but it is true that it embodies a selection from a modest critical harvest rather than a bumper crop.

Let us consider for a space why this should be so. The obvious explanation would be that while time has dealt favorably with Faulkner, Hemingway, and Fitzgerald, its verdict on Dos Passos has been harsher; while his contemporaries have emerged as major writers, Dos Passos has remained a minor one, receiving as much or as little critical attention as he merits. No doubt there are those who would find nothing to question in such a view. But it is possible to be less than wholly satisfied by it. The judgment of time requires time: has enough in fact passed? In the late nineteen twenties, and for most of the thirties, Dos Passos' status was unquestioned: he was accepted as a major figure on the American literary and cultural scene. Nor was his reputation suddenly exploded at some point in the forties, fifties, or sixties; there is no question here of a successful pricking of a bubble reputation, nor of a decisive critical revaluation. Of course it is perfectly true that the new work Dos Passos was producing in these decades received little in the way of favorable critical notice. But there was no damaging suggestion that the decline in the recent work revealed the weaknesses inherent in the earlier. No such case was made. *Manhattan Transfer*, and the trilogy of novels composing *U.S.A.*, survived unscathed, touchstones only of their author's subsequent decline. What seems clear, then, is that a simple appeal to the verdict of time hardly suffices to explain Dos Passos' neglect.

We are left, instead, with an intriguing problem. The major status accorded to Dos Passos in the late twenties and thirties has never been successfully challenged; rather, one's impression is that it has been silently acknowledged. Hence Dos Passos emerges as a more or less standard modern American author about whom, for a considerable period of time, no one—or almost no one—was prepared to write. So much so that in 1951 Arthur Mizener could begin an article in *The Saturday Review of Literature* with the assertion that "During the forties and the fifties John Dos Passos has very nearly achieved the rank of a neglected novelist." [1]

II

To explain that most unlikely phenomenon in American literary historiography—a neglected major author—is a task well worth the serious attention of the cultural historian. In the present context I wish only to offer two brief notes on so extraordinary a situation.

In the first place it may be possible to explain the critical neglect

1. See p. 162 of this volume. Just how right Professor Mizener was is now perfectly clear. In the forties and fifties—and in the sixties—Dos Passos was a neglected novelist at least in the sense that his fiction was subjected to strikingly less of the detailed critical analysis and interpretation so lavishly expended on Faulkner, Hemingway, and Fitzgerald. One piece of statistical evidence is sufficiently revealing. The two-volume Gerstenberger and Hendrick bibliography of twentieth-century criticism of the American novel records its Dos Passos entries in 7 pages. The corresponding figures for Fitzgerald, Hemingway, and Faulkner are, respectively, 17 1/2, 21 1/2, and an astonishing 50 pages.

of Dos Passos on purely aesthetic grounds. What is involved in this connection can be most succinctly indicated by a single question asked, in an essay on Dos Passos written in 1938, by Delmore Schwartz. Attempting to demonstrate the structural inadequacy of *U.S.A.* by appealing to the direct experience of every reader, Mr. Schwartz went on to ask: "What would Henry James say?" [2] What indeed? In terms of the canons established by James, Dos Passos' novels are even looser and baggier monsters than those of George Eliot.

On the face of it, the un-Jamesian quality of the formal structures of Dos Passos' novels should not have mattered very much. Presumably there is room for variety in the kinds of bricks that go to build the house of fiction. But such a view, I believe, underestimates the tightness of the grip on novel criticism exerted by devotees of Jamesian principles, particularly in the period with which we are most concerned: the nineteen forties, fifties, and sixties. Throughout this period the critical debate was conducted along strictly Jamesian lines; it is of felt life, the moral sense, point of view, unreliable narrators, and the rest that we incessantly hear. No doubt novel criticism benefited enormously from its injection of Jamesian stringency. But there were some unhealthy side effects. An important one was the devaluing of a whole area of American fiction: that occupied by those writers who, in American literary history, are described as either "Realists" or "Naturalists." Somewhat unfairly, novelists as diverse as William Dean Howells, Hamlin Garland, Stephen Crane, Frank Norris, Theodore Dreiser—and John Dos Passos—were neglected or rejected because they were assumed to fail the Jamesian test. They contributed nothing to the art of fiction. Even worse, they were suspected of an indiscriminate documentation of life rather than an imaginative and aesthetically satisfying enrichment of it.

Of course one is talking here in the most general terms about the

2. See Delmore Schwartz, "John Dos Passos and the Whole Truth," *Southern Review*, 4 (October 1938), pp. 351–67. Reprinted in J. W. Aldridge, ed., *Critiques and Essays on Modern Fiction* (New York: Ronald Press, 1952). The reference to James occurs on p. 183.

climate of novel criticism. Nonetheless, in relation to Dos Passos, the point is a relevant one. As more than one of the essays included here makes clear, it is a mistake to regard Dos Passos as working exclusively within an American naturalist tradition. Yet his undeniable concern for society as a whole, for the forces at work upon the individual rather than for the individual in his own right, readily explains why he might have been identified with that tradition. So classified, Dos Passos' fiction may well have seemed to lie outside the major concerns of American novel criticism in the nineteen forties, fifties, and sixties.

III

The second note I wish to offer on Dos Passos' neglect is somewhat more uncomfortable in its implications than the first, but any serious sifting of the extant criticism brings some version of it irresistibly forward. In the nineteen twenties and thirties Dos Passos' fiction was discussed and criticized with considerable excitement and passion. Undoubtedly the reason was Dos Passos' radical analysis of American society. Contemporary critics matched the author's radical engagement with their own. What this meant was that the socio-political dimension of Dos Passos' work became a major focus of intellectual and critical concern. It was precisely this dimension which, in the later forties, the fifties, and sixties, may have produced considerable disquiet. Of course, as I have argued, that disquiet was, in part, a question of the dominance of formalist values in novel criticism. But, however regretfully, one suspects the presence of other than aesthetic considerations. Literary criticism is no more immune to the broader forces—economic, religious, political, or whatever—at work within a society than any other form of cultural endeavor. In the period of the Cold War between the United States and the Communist powers, literary radicalism was as unpopular as radicalism of every other kind. What had seemed so exciting in Dos Passos in the twenties and thirties must now have seemed more than a trifle suspect. The safe and sensible answer was to ignore him.

Such a suggestion cannot, by its very nature, be documented. One can appeal only to the general principle of the relationship between culture and society outlined above, and one's own impression of the situation. I find myself, I fear, unable to believe that the absence of American scholarly and critical interest in Dos Passos had no connection whatsoever with the prevailing political ideologies and assumptions of the period in question. Some scholars at least seem to share such a view. In his *Writers on the Left*, Daniel Aaron suggests that "with the Cold War and the crusade of Senator McCarthy, the books and issues of the thirties were considered dangerous as well as dated." [3] Professor Mizener hints at a similar view in an essay written in the mid-sixties in which he suggested that Dos Passos' novels were out of favor for the moment, partly because of the inferiority of his later work, but largely because of a current preference for intensely "private" visions of reality and a concurrent rejection of their past convictions by "one-time intellectual Leftists." [4]

Politics and formalist aesthetics—these then are two areas in which explanations may be sought for Dos Passos' neglect just at the time when the scholarly and critical study of American literature was undergoing a vast, unprecedented expansion. Perhaps there was even a connection between them. Professor Fred Crews suggested just that in a paper he read to the annual meeting of the Modern Language Association in 1969. Professor Crews argued that the formalism characteristic of academic scholarship and criticism in America in the post–World War II period represented an evasion of the social and political issues of the time. (The same case has been made more forcibly in relation to American historical scholarship of the period.) Whether the example of Dos Passos may be seen as supporting this argument or not, the history of Dos Passos criticism undoubtedly does lend substance to another aspect of Professor Crews' argument. Contrasting the committed, engaged quality of much 1930s criticism with "the formalism and static

3. Daniel Aaron, *Writers on the Left* (New York: Harcourt, Brace, 1961), p. 395.
4. Arthur Mizener, *Twelve Great American Novels* (London, Sydney, Toronto: New American Library, 1967), p. 89.

didacticism" of the period which followed, Crews wondered "whether a certain political anguish may not be essential to good criticism." [5] Such a formula provides a challenging explanation of why it is that such critics as Edmund Wilson, Sartre, Lionel Trilling, and Alfred Kazin wrote so well on Dos Passos. Their example at least raises the question of whether our received stance of cool neutrality toward the forms and subjects of imaginative writing is always and necessarily the correct and most fruitful one.

IV

The points I have made go some way toward explaining the pattern of contents within this collection. Criticism from the twenties up to the early forties is heavily represented simply because it was within that period, while his major work was being written, that Dos Passos was most extensively and excitingly discussed. Essays or extracts such as those by Arthur Mizener, Marshall McLuhan, Granville Hicks, and Blanche Gelfant shine out like lonely beacons in the "tranquillized fifties" of Dos Passos criticism. The sixties showed some signs of renewed interest; one or two books on Dos Passos were published, and his name began to appear from time to time in the academic periodicals. In the space available it has not been possible to reflect this new interest quite adequately, but reference may be made to the Selected Bibliography, pp. 185–86.

Three contributions by non-American critics of Dos Passos have been included. That two of these are French and only one English probably reflects accurately the degree of interest shown in Dos Passos in France and Britain. British interest in Dos Passos has never been great, although at the present time, among student readers his reputation seems to be growing. The French, on the other hand, hospitable to all the major American writers of Dos Passos' generation, have always recognized his importance. (It is worth noting that the first book-length study of Dos Passos was published in

5. Frederick Crews, "Do Literary Studies Have an Ideology?" *PMLA*, 85 (May 1970), p. 427.

Paris in 1956 and 1958.) Yet that the one piece of English criticism included should have been written by arguably the greatest, certainly the most influential, of English critics of his generation, is surely not inappropriate. Dr. Leavis, at least, did not fail to recognize in Dos Passos "a serious artist."

It is with Dos Passos' earlier fiction that the majority of critics represented here are concerned. The justification for such an emphasis is of course the overwhelming consensus of critical opinion that Dos Passos' claim to major status rests on *Manhattan Transfer* (1925) and the three novels that make up the *U.S.A.* trilogy: *The 42nd Parallel* (1930), *1919* (1932), and *The Big Money* (1936). Inevitably, therefore, these are the novels that gain most attention. Since it would be both improper and misleading, however, to neglect the novelist's later career entirely, I have included some material which comments on the later novels and at least discounts oversimple "political" explanations of their apparent, relative inferiority.

V

With what Richard Chase has to say about the latter half of Dos Passos' career (pp. 173, 179–80) I find myself in broad agreement. Chase's comments also seem to me to bring the reader close to the heart and soul of Dos Passos' aesthetic and imaginative life. The essential nature of that life emerges reasonably clearly in the course of a letter Dos Passos wrote to Scott Fitzgerald in 1936. The occasion of the letter was the appearance in *Esquire* of Fitzgerald's *Crack-Up* articles, which tried to account for an overwhelming sense of personal frustration and failure. Dos Passos did not try to conceal his exasperation with his friend:

> I've been wanting to see you, naturally, to argue about your *Esquire* articles—Christ, man, how do you find time in the middle of the general conflagration to worry about all that stuff? If you don't want to do stuff on your own, why not get a reporting job somewhere. After all not many people write as well as you do. Here

you've gone and spent forty years in perfecting an elegant and complicated piece of machinery (tool I was going to say) and the next forty years is the time to use it—or as long as the murderous forces of history will let you.[6]

Dos Passos writes here very much in the vein (and imagery) of what in the thirties was described as a "committed" author. For the committed writer it is not the cracking-up of an individual life that is his proper subject; if cracking-up is in question, then it is the cracking-up of a whole world that really matters, the imminent disintegration and dissolution of existing societies and cultures in the face of political power exercised ruthlessly and brutally. In the outbreak of the Spanish Civil War Dos Passos clearly recognized the beginnings of "the general conflagration" which would end by embracing Europe, America, and Asia in the Second World War. Living in what he goes on to describe to Fitzgerald as "one of the damnedest tragic moments in history," Dos Passos could not agree that the artist was adequately fulfilling his role by proceeding in Fitzgerald's manner—that is, by looking inward, by exploring his own inner consciousness. On the contrary, the artist should look outward, recognize the dominant forces at work in society and the world, and struggle to incorporate them within his own imaginative vision. For Dos Passos the final confrontation was not between the artist and his own deepest and truest thinking and feeling self, but between the artist and what he calls "the murderous forces of history."

In that last brilliant phrase, however, lies a suggestion of the origins of commitment as an ideal for the writer. Commitment, which may be broadly defined as the acceptance by a writer of an extra-artistic, usually political, program of action and belief directing his creative endeavors, depends essentially on a romantic view of society and what society represents. One might argue that Pope and Swift, for example, in eighteenth-century England, were just as committed to a vision of the ideal society as any of the writers of the 1930s. But Pope and Swift could write in the belief that theirs

6. F. Scott Fitzgerald, *The Crack-Up* (New York: New Directions Books, 1945), p. 311.

was a collective ideal, one to which all reasonable men would give their assent. No such consonance between individual and social values survived into the nineteenth and twentieth centuries. Indeed one of the recurring meanings of romanticism was precisely a new concern for the individual as individual, outside and independent of society; romantic ideology involved a conscious turning away from society to the individual, both as moral touchstone and as the proper focus of aesthetic attention. The consequence was that social and individual values tended to diverge. And rather than seeing society as, at least ideally, the institutionalized defender of civilized human values, artists came instead to regard the external social world as a vast, unregenerate mass, on the whole hostile to such values.

In this situation how could the artist respond? How could he defend and preserve those values in which he believed? One answer was that of strategic withdrawal. The artist embraced his alienation from society, defined himself as artist precisely by that alienation, and proclaimed the absolute autonomy of art and artistic values. Another answer was counterattack: the artist provided society with images of its own repressiveness and destructiveness and, by so doing, implicitly or explicitly pointed the way to social reformation. The artist who pursued the first course—one which in the end led to the doctrine of art for art's sake—unhesitatingly followed his private vision to the total disregard of any kind of collective or public reality. He was committed, in other words, to the cultivation of the self, the individual sensibility. The artist who followed the second course—the prototype of the committed writer of the thirties —also pursued a private vision; only to realize it he became deeply and centrally engaged, not with individual experience in itself, but with the collective experience of the public world. Neither course resolved the problem of linking private and public worlds—the inner world of the individual sensibility and the outer world of collective social experience.

This was precisely the problem that Dos Passos found himself facing. As he contemplated the fate of the individual in the modern world, and in American society in particular, he came to believe that

reality was not simply what the individual consciousnessness registered or responded to in its surroundings. Reality was rather the
summation of imponderable and impersonal forces, manifest in
terms of history and society, but alien to the experience of the
individual consciousness. But if reality was indeed a vast configuration of impersonal forces experienced collectively rather than individually, the relationship between it and the individual artist was
at once problematical. What kind of relationship could be said to
exist between the individual and collective experience?

For Dos Passos the question was a pressing one. An artist wholly
committed at least to the imaginative recreation of a collectively perceived reality—surely it is significant that one of his recommenda-
tions to Fitzgerald was that he should become a newspaper reporter
—he nevertheless retained a romantic sense of the value of the
individual aesthetic sensibility and an equally romantic view of
the essential hostility of a collective social reality to that sensibility.
Hence his best fiction constantly juxtaposes the two worlds of
private and public experience. The early novels tend to show
how the individual sensibility is inevitably crushed by an impersonal reality. In its portrayal of urban civilization, *Manhattan
Transfer* defines that reality with increased authority and effective-
ness but simultaneously represents an individual protest against it.
U.S.A. charts the movement of history in American society in the
early decades of this century with incomparable power; the ideals
and illusions, the violence, hatreds, and brutalities, the ambitions
and failures of a whole society are all depicted as they are swept
along by the murderous forces of history. Thus it is Dos Passos'
historical sense that seems to determine the range of characters and
events both in the book's narrative sections and elsewhere; it is
what is new, changing, developing, pace-setting, or influential that
preoccupies him. (And this in turn explains why objections to the
"unrepresentative" nature of the picture of American society that
is created are beside the point.) But despite Dos Passos' concern
to identify the trends and forces, the tendencies and movements that
are defining and shaping American society in the twentieth century,
the individual sensibility survives in the world of the trilogy. It

survives directly in the Camera Eye sections, indirectly in the subtle organization and orchestration of the apparent objectivity of the other sections.

U.S.A. nonetheless remains the crucial text for any attempt at penetrating the deep center of Dos Passos' artistic life. The distinctive formal devices of the three novels contribute decisively to their meaning. The Camera Eye, which, despite the ambiguous suggestion of its title, represents, as I have said, the survival within the total fictional world of the individual subjective consciousness, remains formally isolated. The various fictional structures of *U.S.A.*—Newsreels, Biographies, Camera Eye, and narrative sections—are discontinuous. Such a form enacts Dos Passos' sense of the fragmented nature of the individual social and historical experience of modern America. The Camera Eye may allow the individual sensibility a continued existence, but it is an ineffectual existence, cut off from the collective reality that encompasses it. It is as though Dos Passos has been forced to agree that the gap between public and private experience is now unbridgeable. Only the tension between the two survives, in different forms, to provide one of the trilogy's major sources of imaginative power. Perhaps what is wrong with Dos Passos' later fiction is simply that that tension finally disappears: the individual sensibility is subsumed at last within an asserted collective historical experience—however different in its nature from that postulated by the earlier fiction.

Whatever the accuracy of that last surmise, it allows one to make a final point. It is Dos Passos' imaginative rather than political integrity that matters. It is as a creative artist, however committed, not as a political spokesman for left or right, that he must in the end be judged. In Saul Bellow's novel *Henderson the Rain King,* a climax is reached, you may recall, when Henderson struggles heroically to lift up the enormous statue of the goddess Mummah. If we may see Henderson's task as a comic metaphor for that of the artist confronting the overpowering reality of modern America, then the imaginative effort required of him is one before which the majority of Dos Passos' contemporaries and successors have quailed. Yet to achieve as much, to find a form through which America might

be imaginatively lifted up for our aesthetic and passionate contemplation, was the compelling impulse of Dos Passos' art. Whether,
like Henderson, Dos Passos succeeded is the kind of question about
which this volume should promote discussion.

In 1947 Joseph Warren Beach published an essay on Dos Passos,
the general tone of which was decidedly defensive. But Professor
Beach ended on a prophetic note: "Another twenty years and
[Dos Passos] may need no apologia. Our children may positively
relish his flavor and take him for granted as an American classic." [7]
Today, when neither the politics nor the critical values of the recent
past command universal assent, there is no need for apologia. And
it would be pleasant to think that this collection of critical comment,
including as it does views on Dos Passos by some of the ablest critics
of the twentieth century, will indeed help in defining his classic
achievement.

7. See Joseph Warren Beach, "Dos Passos 1947," *Sewanee Review,* 55 (Summer
1947), p. 292.

Dos Passos' Own Views

Some readers may be surprised to find this volume's opening pages given over to the views, not of a critic, but of the author who is its subject. But Dos Passos' views on writing in general, and on his own writing in particular, are sufficiently illuminating to demand inclusion. In 1939 he was one of a large group of American authors who replied to a set of questions, drawn up by the editors of the *Partisan Review,* on what they called "the Situation in American Writing." Here are three of the questions, followed in each case by Dos Passos' answer.

Are you conscious, in your own writing, of the existence of a "usable past"? Is this mostly American? What figures would you designate as elements in it? Would you say, for example, that Henry James's work is more relevant to the present and future of American writing than Walt Whitman's?

JOHN DOS PASSOS. In relation to style and methods of writing, I hardly think of the past in chronological order. Once on the library shelf Juvenal and Dreiser are equally "usable." The best immediate ancestor (in Auden's sense) for today's American writing is I think a dark star somewhere in the constellation containing Mark Twain, Melville, Thoreau and Whitman.

Do you find, in retrospect, that your writing reveals any allegiance to any group, class, organization, region, religion, or system of thought, or do you conceive of it as mainly the expression of yourself as an individual?

JOHN DOS PASSOS. Isn't an individual just a variant in a group? The equipment belongs to the society you were brought up by. The individuality lies in how you use it. My sympathies, for some reason, lie with the private in the front line against the brass hat; with the hodcarrier against the strawboss, or the walking delegate for that matter; with the laboratory worker against the stuffed shirt in a mortarboard; with the criminal against the cop. When I try to use my head it's somewhat different. People are you and me. As for allegiance; what I consider the good side of what's been going on among people on this continent since 1620 or thereabouts, has mine. And isn't there one of history's dusty attics called the Republic of Letters?

How would you describe the political tendency of American writing as a whole since 1930? How do you feel about it yourself? Are you sympathetic to the current tendency towards what may be called "literary nationalism"—a renewed emphasis, largely uncritical, on the specifically "American" elements in our culture?

JOHN DOS PASSOS. On the whole I'm all for the trend towards American self-consciousness in current writing. Of course any good thing gets run into the ground. I think there is enough real democracy in the very mixed American tradition to enable us, with courage and luck, to weather the social transformations that are now going on without losing all our liberties or the humane outlook that is the medium in which civilizations grow. The reaction to home-bred ways of thinking is a healthy defence against the total bankruptcy of Europe. As I have come to believe firmly that in politics the means tend to turn out to be more important than the ends, I think that the more our latent pragmatism and our cynicism in regard to ideas is stimulated the safer we will be.

The Politics of John Dos Passos

by Granville Hicks

Somewhere on the face of the globe there is a bald, near-sighted, stoop-shouldered man in his early fifties, a stocky fellow with a pleasant, slightly apprehensive smile. He could be anywhere; a while back he was writing articles for *Life* from South America, but he may be at his home in Provincetown, or perhaps he is setting off for the Borneo Straits. Wherever he is, John Dos Passos is looking about him with the grim, puzzled honesty that has been his distinctive virtue, almost his trademark, for thirty years.

"All things are changing," the grandson of Charlemagne said, "and we change with them." No American novelist has written more directly about change, the great social changes, the characteristic and revolutionary changes of the twentieth century, than Dos Passos. He has been student and reporter and often poet of change. And he has been the victim of change, too. Twenty years ago he was as romantic a rebel as American letters had seen since the death of John Reed, passionate in his attack on capitalism, quick to support a radical cause. Today this pioneer fellow-traveler defends the profit motive, quarrels not merely with communism but also with the New Deal, looks in dismay at the program of the British Labor Party, and finds in Senator Taft the qualities of leadership he thinks America needs.

In its main parts—infatuation with communism and subsequent disillusionment—the case of Dos Passos is the case of dozens of his contemporaries. Fifty-one of those contemporaries, for instance, joined him in 1932 in signing a statement in support of William Z. Foster, Communist candidate for the presidency. Few of the fifty-one are fellow-travelers today, and several are as intransigently and articulately opposed to the Stalinist regime in Russia as is Dos Passos. The majority of the disillusioned, however, find themselves closer to Norman Thomas or Harry S. Truman than to Senator Taft. The trails of the ex-fellow-travelers go crisscrossing all over the map of American politics, and Dos Passos's is one of the few that lead straight to the right.

There are those who say that he has come to his senses—and high time, too. And there are those who grieve because he has turned into "a weary, cynical defender of vested interests." But few ask how it all happened—the movement to the left and the movement to the right. Yet Dos Passos, being first and foremost a writer, has left a detailed record of what, stage by stage, he has been thinking, and the record is worth looking at, not because he is merely or primarily a political writer but because his political development is a significant phenomenon of our time. I shall not attempt a literary evaluation in this article, nor discuss the problem—more complicated than some of the critics on both the Right and the Left seem to think—of the relationship between Dos Passos's political course and his development as a novelist. This is an attempt to set down the facts and to interpret them on the political level.

The printed record begins in the pages of the *Harvard Monthly* for 1916, when Dos Passos was twenty years old. After having lived in various parts of this country and Europe, he had entered Harvard in 1912, and had soon begun writing for the *Monthly* stories that were a little but not much better than the undergraduate average. It was not, however, until the end of his senior year that he stepped forward as a political thinker, with an editorial on the war and an article entitled "A Humble Protest."

"A Humble Protest" is directed against nothing less than the industrial revolution, "that bastard of science," which is cluttering up the world with "a silly claptrap of unnecessary luxuries" and smothering "the arts of life and the arts of creation." The article offers a dual indictment, moral and esthetic. "Millions of men," Dos Passos writes, "perform labor narrow and stultifying even under the best conditions, bound in the traces of mechanical industry without even a chance of self-expression, except in the hectic pleasures of suffocating lives in cities."

If we were to find that William Faulkner had begun his career with a sweeping attack on industrialism, we should not be surprised, for he has largely devoted himself to the unindustrialized segments of life in the backward South; nor would such a beginning seem inappropriate for the romantic, world-ranging Hemingway or for any of the other novelists who have managed to elude the principal consequences of the industrial revolution. It does startle us to discover that the man who, preeminently among his contemporaries, has refused to dodge industrialism began by repudiating it.

The first World War, in which Dos Passos participated as a member of private ambulance services and of the United States Medical Corps, exhibited to his eyes most of the characteristics he deplored in the civilization that had produced it. It was not blood and death that he wrote about in *One Man's Initiation* and *Three Soldiers,* but tyranny, exploitation, and purposelessness. The tasks of war, as he saw them, were not so much dangerous as "narrow and stultifying," and the destruction of the spirit was worse than the destruction of the flesh. The names that he selected for the sections of *Three Soldiers* established the identity of industrialism and war: "Making the Mould," "The Metal Cools," "Machines," "Rust," and "Under the Wheels."

The war was the first of the critical—one might almost say traumatic—experiences that can be picked out as the turning points of Dos Passos's career. In *One Man's Initiation,* his trial flight, and, much more compellingly, in *Three Soldiers,* he was able to say what kind of shock the war had given him. First of the bitter, disillusioned, unpleasant novels about the war, *Three Soldiers* (1921) was to many readers a blasphemy and an outrage. Coningsby Dawson, author of *The Glory of the Trenches,* wrote in the New York *Times*: "The story is told brutally, with calculated sordidness and a blind whirlwind of rage which respects neither the reticences of art

nor the restraints of decency." But the book was praised by Hey-
wood Broun, Francis Hackett, Sidney Howard, and others, and
eagerly welcomed by the young hopefuls of literature.

"All my life I've struggled for my own liberty in my small way,"
says Martin Howe, the hero of *One Man's Initiation*. "Now I hardly
know if the thing exists." That, of course, was the lesson of the war.
Like young Howe, Dos Passos had fought against "all the conven-
tional ties, the worship of success and the respectabilities that is
drummed into you when you're young." And the battle had not
gone too badly; one could even write in the *Harvard Monthly* that
industrialism was a mistake and civilization was on the wrong road.
But he had underestimated the strength of the enemy. The enemy
could pick you up and put you into uniform, wipe out your individuality, make you part of the machine.

Yet *Three Soldiers,* for all its bitterness, is essentially a hopeful
book, as Dos Passos remembered when, in 1932, he wrote an introduction for the Modern Library edition: "Any spring is a time of
overturn, but then (1919) Lenin was alive, the Seattle strike had
seemed the beginning of the flood instead of the beginning of the
ebb, Americans in Paris were groggy with theatre and painting and
music; Picasso was to rebuild the eye, Stravinski was cramming the
Russian steppes into our ears, currents of energy seemed breaking
out everywhere as young guys climbed out of their uniforms, im-
perial America was all shiny with the new idea of Ritz, in every
direction the countries of the world stretched out starving and
angry, ready for anything turbulent and new, whenever you went to
the movies you saw Charlie Chaplin." The sufferings and defeats
he depicted in *Three Soldiers* were made doubly black because they
were silhouetted against the flaming hopes of the spring of 1919.

Chrisfield, one of the three soldiers, asks Andrews out of his desperation if it would be possible to overthrow the government. Andrews, who stands closest to the author, answers, "They did in
Russia. We'll see." If, on the one hand, the war had shown Dos
Passos the sheer repressive strength of organized society, it had, on
the other, revealed the existence of unsuspected and powerful movements of revolt. *One Man's Initiation* is full of the heady talk of

French anarchists and socialists, and if *Three Soldiers* portrays the failure of individual revolt, it holds out, however cryptically, the hope of collective revolution.

It took Dos Passos a long time to come to terms with his war experiences, five or six years. He wrote a book of verse and a bad novel, and he traveled. Always, when he has been unsure of himself, he has traveled. In Spain and the Near East he noted with discouragement the progress of "Henry Ford's gospel of multiple production and interchangeable parts," bringing the whole world to "the same level of nickel-plated dullness." He had fun from time to time, but wherever he went and whatever he was doing, he kept his mind on the problem he had made his own, the problem of living in an industrialized world. He was a serious-minded, conscientious fellow, not much like Ernest Hemingway, who could forget *his* preoccupations in drinking or hunting or skiing or watching a bullfight. He thought he wanted to escape, but he couldn't. And perhaps he didn't really want to. There is a passage in *Orient Express* that comes up suddenly and hits you in the eye. Dos Passos is in his hotel room in Kasvin, Persia, and he is bored. "It is in the West," he thinks abruptly, "that blood flows hot and that the world is disorderly, romantic, that fantastic unexpected things happen. Here everything has been tried, experienced, worn out." He wishes himself—where? At Broadway and 42nd Street.

And that is where, in a manner of speaking, we next see him, when his *Wanderjahre* are over and he is settling down to write *Manhattan Transfer*. If he had always hated industrial, urban civilization, he had also been fascinated by it, and now he admits its fascination. *Manhattan Transfer* is a poem of hate-and-love. The hatred is underlined on every page: for the ruthlessness, the fraudulence, the sycophancy, and the treachery that mark the struggle for success; for the emptiness and the inhumanity of the successful; for the folly and ineffectualness of those who fail in an unworthy cause. But the world Dos Passos portrays is disorderly and romantic, and the things that happen are fantastic, unexpected, and fun to write about. "Why," asks Jimmy Herf, the deracinated intellectual who is as central a character as this deliberately amorphous novel can be

expected to have, "why do I go on dragging out a miserable existence in this crazy epileptic town?" But he does, for many pages after
the question has been asked, and his ultimate departure is made to
seem as hazardous and portentous as the escape from an enchanted
castle in a fairy story.

There is not much politics in *Manhattan Transfer*; the book is
directed against a way of life, not a political or economic system—
against greed and conformity and pretentiousness. It is not, however,
calculated to inculcate respect for the qualities that bring success
under capitalism, and no reader could suppose that Dos Passos had
been reconciled to the capitalist system. In fact, he was affiliating
himself with the avowed enemies of capitalism. In 1926, the year
after *Manhattan Transfer* was published, he became a member of
the executive board of the *New Masses,* which was launched with
the aid of a subsidy from the Garland Fund. Although the venture
received the support of many of the individualistic rebels who had
contributed to the old *Masses,* the communists, as Dos Passos must
have known, were running the show.

Dos Passos contributed many short articles and book reviews to
early issues of the *New Masses,* but the most interesting of his contributions, and the one that shows how far he was in 1926 from communist or any other kind of orthodoxy, was a debate with Mike
Gold on the subject of the magazine itself. He begins, in characteristic fashion, by discussing the special limitations of the writing business. The writer, he says, "takes on the mind and functional de-
formities of his trade," no matter what his ideas and aims. "The
word-slinging organism is the same whether it sucks its blood from
Park Avenue or from Flatbush." The magazine will succeed only if it
keeps clear of dogmas, imported or domestic. "The terrible danger
to explorers," he goes on, "is that they always find what they are
looking for. The *American Mercury* explores very ably the American
field only to find the face of Mr. Mencken mirrored in every prairie
pool." What he would like to see is "a magazine full of introspec-
tion and doubt that would be like a piece of litmus paper to test
things by."

Mike Gold, a loyal communist and in those days a conspicuous one, was horrified by such heresies. "Dos Passos," he wrote, "must read history, psychology and economics and plunge himself into the labor movement. He must ally himself definitely with the radical army, for in this struggle is the only true escape from middle-class bewilderment today." Dos Passos did not precisely follow Gold's advice, but we do find him writing on the Passaic strike, discussing the economic causes of war, and describing with ardent approval the revolutionary art of Mexico.

Dos Passos, however, was bound to find his own battles and fight them his own way. The ordeal of Sacco and Vanzetti was nearing its tragic climax, and Dos Passos devoted more and more of his time to work for the release of the two Italian anarchists. The pamphlet he wrote for the Sacco-Vanzetti Defense Committee, "Facing the Chair," is factual and calm, but Dos Passos himself was moved as he had not been in many years. He went to Boston the week of the execution, picketed in company with Mike Gold, Dorothy Parker, Edna St. Vincent Millay, and many others, and spent a night in jail. What he felt he put into words nearly ten years later, when some of his political theories had changed but the emotion remained sharp and unaltered in his memory. It is in *The Big Money*: "they have clubbed us off the streets they are stronger they are rich. . . . America our nation has been beaten by strangers who have turned our language inside out who have taken the clean words our fathers spoke and made them slimy and foul." He sums up: "all right, we are two nations."

The electrocution of Sacco and Vanzetti was another of Dos Passos's traumatic experiences. Like so many idealists, he had not believed that it could happen, had been convinced to the end that justice and decency had to prevail. He was not being literary—and certainly not chauvinistic—when he talked about strangers. That was the way it seemed to him; the people who had "bought the laws and fenced off the meadows and cut down the woods for pulp and turned our pleasant cities into slums and sweated the wealth out of our people" were spiritual aliens, nurtured in a different tradition from that on which America was built. They were interlopers, usurpers, bandits, and they must be driven out. In a confused and crowded play that he wrote just after the death of Sacco and Vanzetti, *Airways, Inc.,* he examined for the first time the dialectics of fighting fire with fire.

Dos Passos visited Russia in the autumn of 1928, and his impressions, though considerably short of rapture, were favorable enough to be published in the *New Masses.* Anyone might have known, however, that he could come to communism only by an American route, and his observations in the Soviet Union seem to have had little influence, one way or the other, on his thinking. When, shortly after his return from Russia, he sat down to begin *The 42nd Parallel,* first volume of the trilogy *U.S.A.,* he accepted the basic Marxist conception of the class struggle, but it was not an idea he had picked up in the USSR or, for that matter, acquired from the reading of Marx. His observations, especially in the matter of Sacco and Vanzetti, had taught him what he knew about the two nations.

Sooner than most Americans, including the orthodox communists, Dos Passos saw the implications of the depression that began in 1929. The class war, he realized, had actually begun, and he wrote articles, both in the *New Republic* and the *New Masses,* urging middle-class liberals to make sure that the struggle was conducted "under the most humane conditions possible." This was a novel suggestion to come from a fellow-traveler, and the suspicious communists promptly denounced it as wishy-washy liberalism. In time, however, they perceived that Dos Passos, whatever his motives, was tactically sound, and the "neutralizing" of the middle class became a major communist aim.

What Dos Passos was seeking was a compromise between his liberal, humanitarian traditions and his communist sympathies, but, in spite of his intellectual reservations, his practical activity was directed into communist channels. He helped to organize the Emergency Committee for Southern Prisoners, and later was chairman of the National Committee to Aid Striking Miners Fighting Starvation. In the autumn of 1931 he and Theodore Dreiser and half a dozen other writers went to Harlan County, Kentucky, to call attention to the violation of civil rights in a communist-led strike. He was one of the founders and for several years the treasurer of the National Committee for the Defense of Political Prisoners, and he was active in the Scottsboro case and in other cases in which the communists took an acutely political interest. As had been noted, he was one of fifty-two writers and artists who signed a statement in support of the communist candidates in the 1932 election.

In that summer of 1932, V. F. Calverton, editor of the *Modern Monthly,* asked various literary figures some tendentious questions, among them, "Should a writer join the Communist Party?" Dos Passos replied: "It's his own goddam business. Some people are naturally party men and others are natural scavengers and campfollowers. Matter of temperament. I personally belong to the scavenger and campfollower section." This was obviously true, and yet Dos Passos was rendering a more valuable service to the Communist Party at just that time than most of its members, for his prestige was great and his sincerity unchallenged. No one had more influence on the leftward swing of the intellectuals in the early 30's.

His growing militancy naturally affected his writing, and *1919,* second volume of his trilogy, gave a sharper sense of revolutionary crisis than *The 42nd Parallel.* What Dos Passos was feeling appeared most strikingly in the biographies: the sympathetic portrayals of the radicals, Jack Reed, Randolph Bourne, Paxton Hibben, Joe Hill, and Wesley Everest; the mordant accounts of Theodore Roosevelt, Woodrow Wilson, and Pierpont Morgan; the indignant, touching poem about the Unknown Soldier. As for the characters of the story, most of them—Eveline Hutchins, Eleanor Stoddard, Ward Moorehouse, Dick Savage, Jerry Burnham, and so on—illustrate the disintegration and emptiness of the middle class. The one worker, Joe Williams, is not romanticized, but he is handled respectfully, and in the latter part of the book we have a bona fide revolutionary, also treated with respect, Ben Compton. Most of the leftwing reviewers observed, with varying degrees of leftwing snobbishness, that Dos Passos was scarcely a bona fide revolutionary, but they felt that he was on the way.

Dos Passos in 1932 was closer to communism than he had ever been—and as close as he was going to get. In his parabolic orbit, though he did not know it, he had reached perihelion. For a time

nothing much happened. Although he was less active in 1933 than
he had been in 1931 and 1932, he continued to belong to a lot of
communist fronts, and when the *New Masses* became a weekly at
the beginning of 1934, he was advertised as one of its principal contributors. He did contribute a couple of articles, but the alliance
lasted only a few weeks. In February, the Socialist Party held a rally
in Madison Square Garden to protest against the suppression of the
socialist workers of Vienna. In the name of the united front, communists invaded the meeting, which ended in a first-class riot, with
a blow-by-blow account going out on the radio. A letter criticizing
the behavior of the Communist Party on this occasion was sent to
the *New Masses,* signed by Dos Passos and twenty-four others. ("We
who write this letter watch with sympathy the struggles of militant
labor and aid such struggles.") The *New Masses* answered with a
letter addressed to Dos Passos, which weakly defended communist
actions at the Garden and strongly attacked the signers of the letter.
Some of the signers, the *New Masses* said, were well-known Trotskyite troublemakers, and others had given little evidence of their sympathy with militant labor. In a fervent peroration the editors ob-
jected to being addressed as "Dear Comrades" by such renegades
and stoolpigeons. "You," the editorial concluded, "are different. To
us, you have been, and, we hope, still are, Dos Passos the revolutionary writer, the comrade."

If Dos Passos had not already had some doubts about communist
tactics, the Garden riot could not have hit him so hard, but it was
a peculiarly flagrant example of the brutal literalness with which the
party line could be applied. The same tactics had betrayed the striking miners in Kentucky and split the anti-fascist movement in Germany. Dos Passos had seen enough. He did not contribute to the
New Masses again, and he ceased to work with communist fronts.
For the time being, he issued no denunciations of communism, but
his disillusionment was great and it grew rapidly.

Out of his dual disillusionment, the old quarrel with capitalism
and the new distrust of communism, he wrote *The Big Money,* and
thus completed his trilogy. Again the key is in the biographies:
Frederick W. Taylor, Henry Ford, Thorstein Veblen, Isadora Dun-

can, Rudolph Valentino, the Wright brothers, Frank Lloyd Wright, William Randolph Hearst, and Samuel Insull. It is all a Veblenian world: "the sabotage of production by business, the sabotage of life by blind need for money profits." The Veblenian moral is driven home by the story of Charley Anderson, which occupies the greater part of the novel. "If you're workin' with us, you're workin' with us," says Old Bledsoe, who is in charge of production in the Detroit airplane factory for which Charley goes to work, "and if you're not you'd better stick around your broker's office where you belong." Charley means well, but "the blind need for money profits" takes him to his broker's office and eventually to his death. Everyone, indeed, ends badly in *The Big Money*—the revolutionaries as well as the capitalists and their hangers-on. There is no optimism, no militancy, and, for that matter, no tragedy—just the sour taste of frustration and futility.

The Big Money was published in 1936. That summer General Franco and his fascists began their revolt against the republican government of Spain, and in America radical and liberal opinion was solidly on the side of the Loyalists. Dos Passos had been in Spain in 1916, 1920, and 1933, and in 1937 he went again, one of his purposes being to collaborate with the cameraman Joris Ivens in the filming of a pro-Loyalist picture called *Spanish Earth*. Dos Passos' sympathy for the Loyalist cause came out clearly enough in what he wrote about the civil war, but his articles didn't quite have the fervor to be found in reports by Ernest Hemingway and others. In Stalinist circles in America, the word went round that Dos had fallen under the spell of anarchists and Trotskyites. Only later was it learned that a friend of his, a Spaniard who had taught at Johns Hopkins University and had been an officer in the Loyalist army, had been arrested by secret police and mysteriously executed.

Dos Passos could speak two years later of the death of José Robles Pazos as "only one story among thousands in the vast butchery that was the Spanish civil war," but it seems to have been at the time another of his traumatic experiences. In *Adventures of a Young Man,* the hero, a disillusioned communist, goes to fight in Spain out of a conviction that here is the final conflict, the real fight against reaction, transcending all sectarian feuds. But this young man, Glenn Spotswood, is arrested by a GPU agent, accused of Trotskyism, and sent to his death. In Spain Dos Passos had concluded that communism was not merely something he could not support; it was as much the enemy as fascism or any other brand of reaction.

Even in 1937, there were plenty of ex-fellow-travelers to agree with Dos Passos, though more of them had been disillusioned by the trials of the Old Bolsheviks than by events in Spain. And there were plenty more by the end of 1939, after the Soviet-Nazi pact and the liquidation of the democratic front. Although the erstwhile communists and communist-sympathizers were well distributed over the political map, as has been said, the majority of them were concentrated in support of the New Deal, and that was where Dos Passos seemed to be taking his stand. Both in *Adventures of a Young Man* and in an article he published in 1941, "To a Liberal in Office," he admitted that he had been wrong in his earlier, leftwing criticisms of the New Deal, which, he said, "in spite of many wrong roads taken," has been "productive of real living good in the national life." *The Ground We Stand On,* a study of some of the founders of American democracy, has a New Dealish air, and the second volume of the Spotswood trilogy, *Number One,* a novel about someone like Huey Long, also seemed to belong in the New Deal tradition.

In an interview he gave in the winter of 1949, after *The Grand Design* had been published, Dos Passos said he was surprised that reviewers had regarded the book as an all-out attack on the New Deal; "It was Mr. Roosevelt's foreign—not domestic—policy that disappointed him." As anyone who has read the novel knows, the reviewers could scarcely be blamed, and yet it was true that Dos Passos had not quarreled with the New Deal in the years before Pearl Harbor. What is even more surprising, he appeared to support Roosevelt's foreign policy between 1941 and 1945. At any rate, *State of the Nation,* a collection of magazine pieces published in 1944, is critical only of details, not of general policies, and so sharp-eyed a critic as Edmund Wilson concluded from it that Dos Passos, however reluctantly, favored the prosecution of the war.

But Dos Passos could not have supported either the New Deal or the war without serious misgivings. Nothing is deeper in the man than his fear of power. To begin with, he feared the power of the military, as he had experienced it in the first World War, and the power of men of wealth. The hatred of war and exploitation grew so acute that he accepted for a time the tempting radical doctrine that only power can destroy power. But what he saw of communism in Russia, in Spain, and at home convinced him that the destroying power could be more dangerous than the power it overcame. The New Deal, whatever its accomplishments, represented a great concentration of power, and he must always have been uneasy about it. As for war, Dos Passos hated it in and for itself and because it inevitably resulted in the piling of power upon power.

The misgivings do not figure much in *State of the Nation* or the first part of *Tour of Duty*. (Dos Passos has always been a first-rate reporter, and from these books, less ballyhooed than many of the wartime quickies and as promptly forgotten, future historians will learn things they cannot find elsewhere.) But his uneasiness was preparing the way for a sudden reversal, and it came, as Part III of *Tour of Duty* shows, when he visited Austria and Germany in the autumn of 1945. "In the Year of Our Defeat" he called this section, arguing that we had been defeated in two ways: we had callously surrendered the peoples of eastern Europe to Russian despotism, and we had no intelligent, humane plan for the reconstruction of the occupied countries. The destruction America had wrought was before his eyes, and its apparent futility stabbed his tender conscience.

Something, he saw, had gone wrong, and his conscience said, "I told you so." He should always have known that no good could come of war, should have seen from the first that no man could exercise the power that had been entrusted to Franklin D. Roosevelt without abusing it. Dos Passos looked at the postwar world and was afraid, more afraid than he had ever been in his life.

Out of his fear he wrote *The Grand Design*. He did not intend it to be a diatribe against the New Deal, but that is what it became. There are "good" New Dealers in the book, but they are defeated by the charlatans and demagogues, by the ineffable Walker Watson, who combines the worst traits of Henry Wallace and Harry Hopkins, by Jerry Evans, the insatiable millionaire from the South, and by the "indispensable" man in the White House. "By the modulations of his voice on the microphone he played on the American people. We danced to his tune. Third Term. Fourth Term. Indispensable. War is a time of Caesars."

The moral of the book is given in one of the quasi-poetic passages with which it is sprinkled:

> We learned. There were things we learned to do but we have not learned, in spite of the Constitution and the Declaration of Independence and the great debates at Richmond and Philadelphia how to put power over the lives of men into the hands of one man and to make him use it wisely.

This is as true as anything can be, but it is also true that we have not learned how to get along at this stage of the development of Western Civilization without putting power over the lives of men into the hands of one man. The dangers are great, and Dos Passos is not the only one who sees them. At the end of *Roosevelt and Hopkins,* Robert Sherwood expresses the hope that the nation will never again find it necessary to place "so much reliance on the imagination and the courage and the durability of one mortal man." But unfortunately the perception of a danger does not automatically provide a way of avoiding it.

"Socialism is not the answer to the too great concentration of power that is the curse of capitalism. We've got to do better than that." So Dos Passos wrote in "The Failure of Marxism," published in *Life* Magazine in early 1948. But the article, instead of being concerned with the "better than that," complains peevishly that such phrases as "public ownership" and "planned economy" have acquired a favorable connotation, apparently through the operations of some sinister conspiracy, and proceeds to run through the stock objections to socialization with as little originality as a National Association of Manufacturers' leaflet. Dos Passos' horrible examples include not only Russian tyranny but also British Labor bureaucracy. He sees the British government's "direction of labor" measure not as a temporary expedient nor even as a mistake that can be corrected through the democratic procedures that do, after all, survive in England, but as a step that will inevitably lead to totalitarianism. The evils of capitalism, though they are occasionally mentioned, seem scarcely worth bothering with.

Dos Passos is not, of course, a defender of vested interests. On the contrary, his sympathies are wholly with the people who get pushed around, whether it is Big Business or Big Government that does the pushing. His trouble is simply that he has not found the "better than that," the alternative to both bignesses, and hence his growing fear of government can only be accompanied by a growing toleration of business. ("The untrammeled power of the ruling class in the Soviet Union makes you wonder whether the profit motive is as bad as it has been painted.") He has allowed himself to be forced into choosing one horn of the dilemma, and he is nicely impaled.

In the article that he wrote for the *Harvard Monthly* more than thirty years ago, Dos Passos argued that the industrial revolution was a mistake, that history had taken the wrong turning. In his recent writing this concept of the wrong turning still devils him, though he now conceives of it in political terms. At some point, he appears to be saying, we in this country wantonly surrendered our heritage of liberty and thus plunged ourselves into all our difficulties. We must go back to that point, if we can find it, and start off again on the true course.

This is one way of reading history, and for some purposes it may have its validity, but it does not provide much guidance for realistic action in the immediate situation. It is strange that Dos Passos, who shied away from Marxist dogmatism when he was close to the Communist Party, who remained far more flexible and open-minded than most of the fellow-travelers, has now stumbled into a kind of absolutism. If, for instance, he sees that the New Deal was in part an evil, he cannot bring himself to say that it may have been a lesser evil. It is not enough for him to condemn the abuse of power; he must condemn power itself.

When Edmund Wilson reviewed *State of the Nation* in 1944, he remarked that the world had moved away from Dos Passos and that his imagination was not involved with his material as it had been when he was at his best. Today, even more than five years ago, he seems dissociated from the kind of reality he has chosen to deal with. Perhaps it is not merely metaphorical to talk about traumatic experiences; perhaps he is a victim of the successive shocks he has undergone. If the shocks had driven him in upon himself, they might have deepened his work, but he has remained committed, as few American novelists have been, to the portrayal and interpretation of the impersonal, the historic event. Everything has depended on his maintaining a vital relationship to the outer world, and a break in that relationship was bound to result not only in political confusion but also in a decline of literary mastery.

But he goes on seeking, and who knows what he may yet find? If there are some things he has lost, courage, honesty, and a fundamental generosity of spirit remain. He has been a true explorer in his day, and may be again, since nothing has crushed the will to understand.

Dos Passos and the Social Revolution

by Edmund Wilson

John Dos Passos's *Airways, Inc.,* was produced in March as the last play of the second season of the New Playwrights' Theater, and almost entirely failed to attract attention. This was due, principally, I believe, to the fact that by that time the critics had become rather discouraged with the revolutionary drama of Grove Street and that the New Playwrights themselves were so low in funds that they could not afford proper publicity. None the less, *Airways, Inc.,* was a remarkable play, perhaps the best that the New Playwrights have done; and though this is not the place to speak of the merits of the Grove Street production, which I thought were considerable, the published text of the play demands attention as a work of literature.

Airways is, like the group's other plays, a social-political-economic fable; but Dos Passos is more intelligent than most of his associates —he is able to enter into more points of view—and he is a much better artist. His play is neither a naturalistic study nor a vaudeville in the manner of John Howard Lawson, though it has some of the elements of both; it is rather a sort of dramatic poem of contemporary America. With great ingenuity, Dos Passos had assembled on a single suburban street-corner representatives of most of the classes and groups that go to make up our society. We concentrate upon the life of a single middle-class household, but this is submerged in a larger world: its fate is inextricably bound up with a current real-estate boom; a strike that eventually gives rise to a Sacco-Vanzetti

"Dos Passos and the Social Revolution." From *Shores of Light* by Edmund Wilson (New York: Farrar, Straus & Giroux, Inc., 1952), pp. 429-35. Reprinted with the permission of Farrar, Straus & Giroux, Inc. Copyright 1952 by Edmund Wilson.

31

incident; and the promotion of a commercial aviation company. Nor, as is likely to be the case in this kind of play, are the social types merely abstractions which never persuade the imagination. Dos Passos has succeeded in producing the illusion that behind the little suburban street-corner of the Turners lies all the life of a great American city—all the confusion of America itself; and *Airways* made the meager stage of the bleak little Grove Street Theater seem as big as any stage I have ever seen. Dos Passos has also given the household of the Turners an extension in time as well as in space: he has provided a chorus of two old men, an American inventor and a Hungarian revolutionist, whose role is to relate what we see to what has gone before in history and to what may be expected to come after.

It is in the construction of this sort of sociological fable that Dos Passos particularly excels. The strength of his novel, *Manhattan Transfer,* lay in the thoroughness and the steady hand with which he executed a similar anatomy on the city of New York as a whole. As a dramatist he is less expert; and *Airways* suffers in certain ways from comparison with *Manhattan Transfer.* Dos Passos sometimes interrupts his action with long passages of monologue, which, though they might go down easily in a novel, discourage our attention in the theater; and his last act, though the two separate scenes are excellent in themselves, fails to draw the different strands together as we expect a third act to do. But, on the other hand, *Airways,* at its best, has an eloquence and a spirit that *Manhattan Transfer* largely lacked. It is one of the best-written things that Dos Passos has so far done—perhaps freer than any other of his productions both from rhetoric doing duty for feeling and from descriptions too relentlessly piled up. Dos Passos is probably only now arriving at his mature prose style.

So much for the purely artistic aspect of *Airways.* It is impossible to discuss it further without taking into account Dos Passos's political philosophy. Dos Passos is, one gathers from his work, a social revolutionist: he believes that, in the United States as elsewhere, the present capitalistic regime is destined to be overthrown by a class-conscious proletariat. And his disapproval of capitalist society seems to imply a distaste for all the beings who go to compose it. In *Man-*

hattan Transfer, it was not merely New York, but humanity that came off badly. Dos Passos, in exposing the diseased organism, had the effect, though not, I believe, the intention, of condemning the sufferers along with the disease; and even when he seemed to desire to make certain of his characters sympathetic, he had a way of putting them down.

Now, in *Airways,* there are several characters whom Dos Passos has succeeded in making either admirable or attractive, but these are, in every case, either radicals or their sympathizers. His bias against the economic system is so strong that it extends beyond its official representatives to all those human beings whose only fault is to have been born where such a system prevails and to be so lacking in courage or perspicacity as not to have allied themselves with the forces that are trying to fight it. In Dos Passos, not only must the policeman not fail to steal the money with which the street-kids have been playing craps; but even the young people of *Airways* who, however irresponsible and immoral, might be expected to exhibit something of the charm of youth—become uglier and uglier as the play proceeds, till they finally go completely to pieces in a drunken restaurant scene which is one of Dos Passos's masterpieces of corrosive vulgarity. It is especially curious to note the treatment which the American aviators receive at the hands of both Dos Passos and Lawson. The aviator is one of the authentic heroes that our American civilization now produces. But for Lawson or Dos Passos, an aviator cannot be an authentic hero, or even, apparently, a genius, because he is not on the side of the revolution. The truth is, of course, that the aviator of the type of Lindbergh or Byrd never troubles himself with these questions at all and, even when, as in the case of Lindbergh, he is exploited for a time by the government, he exists and performs his achievements in a world independent of politics. But to a Lawson or a Dos Passos, he is suspect: they cannot let him get away with anything, and eventually, in what they write, they succeed in destroying or degrading him. In Lawson's play, *The International,* another New Playwrights production, the Lindbergh character appears as a drunken taxi-driver—or perhaps as a drunken bum in a taxi—amid the débâcle of the capitalist state; and in *Airways,* the young aviator is sent up by the agents of his capitalist employers to scatter leaflets on a strikers' meeting. He is drunk, and falls and breaks his back.

Now, the life of middle-class America, even under capitalism and even in a city like New York, is not so unattractive as Dos Passos makes it—no human life under any conditions can ever have been so unattractive. Under however an unequal distribution of wealth, human beings are still capable of enjoyment, affection and enthusiasm—even of integrity and courage. Nor are these qualities and emotions entirely confined to class-conscious workers and their leaders. There are moments in reading a novel or seeing a play by Dos Passos when one finds oneself ready to rush to the defense of even the American bathroom, even the Ford car—which, after all, one begins to reflect, have perhaps done as much to rescue us from helplessness, ignorance and squalor as the prophets of revolution. We may begin to reflect upon the relation, in Dos Passos, of political opinions to artistic effects. Might it not, we ask ourselves, be possible —have we not, in fact, seen it occur—for a writer to hold Dos Passos's political opinions and yet not depict our middle-class republic as a place where no birds sing, no flowers bloom and where the very air is almost unbreathable? For, in the novels and plays of Dos Passos, everybody loses out: if he is on the right side of the social question, he has to suffer, if he is not snuffed out; if he is on the oppressors' side, his pleasures are made repulsive. When a man as intelligent as Dos Passos—that is, a man a good deal more intelligent than, say, Michael Gold or Upton Sinclair, who hold similar political views—when so intelligent a man and so good an artist allows his bias so to falsify his picture of life that, in spite of all the accurate observation and all the imaginative insight, its values are partly those of melodrama—we begin to guess some stubborn sentimentalism at the bottom of the whole thing, some deeply buried streak of hysteria of which his misapplied resentments represent the aggressive side. And from the moment we suspect the process by which he has arrived at his political ideas, the ideas themselves become suspect.

In the meantime, whatever diagnosis we may make of Dos Passos's infatuation with the social revolution, he remains one of the few first-rate figures among our writers of his generation, and the only one of these who has made a systematic effort to study all the aspects of America and to take account of all its elements, to compose them into a picture which makes some general sense. Most of the first-rate men of Dos Passos's age—Hemingway, Wilder, Fitzgerald—cultivate their own little corners and do not confront the situation as a whole. Only Dos Passos has tried to take hold of it. In the fine last speech of *Airways*, he allows the moral of his play to rise very close to the surface. The spinster sister of the Turner household has just received the news that the strike leader, with whom she has been in love and who has been made the victim of a frame-up, has finally been electrocuted: "Now I'm beginning to feel it," she says, "the house without Walter, the street without him, the city without him, the future that we lived in instead of a honeymoon without him, everything stark without him. Street where I've lived all these years shut up in a matchwood house full of bitterness. City where I've lived walled up in old dead fear. America, where I've scurried from store to subway to church to home, America that I've never known. World where I've lived without knowing. What can I do now that he is gone and that he has left me full of scalding wants, what can I do with the lack of him inside me like a cold stone? The house I lived in wrecked, the people I loved wrecked, around me there's nothing but words stinging like wasps. Where can I go down the dark street, where can I find a lover in the sleeping city? At what speed of the wind can I fly away, to escape these words that burn and sting, to escape the lack that is in me like a stone?"

It is true that the lack of real leadership is felt by us today as a stone. It is Dos Passos's recognition of this—his relentless reiteration of his conviction that there is something lacking, something wrong, in America—as well as his insistence on the importance of America —that gives his work its validity and power. It is equally true, of course, of H. L. Mencken that he finds something lacking and something wrong; but the effect of Mencken on his admirers is to make them wash their hands of social questions. Mencken has made it the fashion to speak of politics as an obscene farce. And Dos Passos is now almost alone among the writers of his generation in continuing to take the social organism seriously.

John Dos Passos: The Synoptic Novel

by Blanche H. Gelfant

The Novelist as "Architect of History"

John Dos Passos' *Manhattan Transfer,* first hailed by Sinclair Lewis as a germinal work and called by Joseph Warren Beach "one of the most brilliant and original American novels of the century," [1] holds a unique place in American city fiction. The finest example of the synoptic form of the city novel, it is one of the most ambitious experiments in the use of urban materials. Perhaps no other city novel reveals such sheer virtuosity in the handling of urban imagery and symbolism, such skill in creating the city as an entity in itself, and such ingenuity in making a complex form the vehicle of implicatory social commentary. In its search for techniques to project the city immediately, in all its dazzling and stupefacient variety, in its sensuous shapes and aesthetic moments, its pace, rhythms, and atmosphere, *Manhattan Transfer* becomes a kind of text on the art of the city novel. Yet the achievement of *Manhattan Transfer* is not only its brilliant and imaginative creation of modern New York as an immediate place: its achievement is also its serious social and moral interpretation of a twentieth-century way of life. Underlying the aesthetics of the novel is a concept of the novelist as an "architect of history"—a shaper of moral opinion who influences the group mind of his times by compelling and revealing works of art. The total achievement of *Manhattan*

1. Joseph Warren Beach, *The Twentieth-Century Novel: Studies in Technique* (New York, The Century Company, 1932), 437.

Transfer as city fiction must be evaluated in terms of Dos Passos' peculiar concept of the novelist's function, a concept that determined the historical sweep of the novel, the direct focusing upon the city rather than upon its people, and the underlying interpretation of Manhattan as a huge symbol of twentieth-century historical tendencies.

In various essays, prefaces, and letters (almost all written in the thirties), Dos Passos expressed his views on the relationship between social history and literature, between the writer's moral responsibility to his times and his search for a technique. Underlying these views was an urgent sense of the dynamics of social change—specifically, a feeling that America was standing at a historical crossroad. As he expressed it in one essay (the idea is also stated in *U.S.A.* in the biographical sketch of Veblen): "This is an epoch of sudden and dangerous transition. Industrial life is turning a corner and is either going to make the curve or smash up in the ditch." [2]

The sense that he was living through a crucial period of deep-reaching historical change was given theoretical validity by the dialectical formula of Marx. Marxian theory defined history as a dynamic process in which one social system and its forms gave way to another. But abstract theory stood confirmed for Dos Passos by his personal observations of social change in America and "in all countries"—in Spain, Russia, South America, Mexico, and the Orient. These observations are recorded in his early travel books, *Rosinante to the Road Again* and *In All Countries*. It is a mistake to consider these books wistful expressions of Dos Passos' early escapism, for they reveal him actually as a concerned and alerted social observer, sensitive to symptoms of social evolution everywhere and particularly interested in the mechanisms of revolution. While revolution brought violent and abrupt social change to Russia and Mexico, a slow evolutionary process was bringing it to Spain. Dos Passos evaluated the change in Spain (as industrialism encroached upon an ancient agricultural way of life) in terms of the past. Always he brought to bear upon the present a keen nostalgic sense of

2. John Dos Passos, "Why Write for the Theatre Anyway?" Introduction to *Three Plays* (New York, Harcourt, Brace and Company, 1934), xx.

the past. Perhaps the past as he envisioned it was idealized, never having been really as generous to the individual nor as culturally rich as he liked to think. But the awareness of the past as an idealistic point of reference influenced his judgment of the contemporary scene.

When he looked upon America of the twenties and thirties, he evoked an image of a Jeffersonian past in which democratic ideals had been instituted as a way of life. These ideals seemed to him under deliberate assault in twentieth-century America. They were attacked directly during and by World War I. He said himself that he had been unable to reconcile the "brutalities" and "oppressions" of the war with the ideals of progress he had been led to believe in.[3] The war seemed to him a "horrible monstrosity."[4] He shared the general disillusionment of his generation which had come to regard the war as (to use his character Joe Williams' phrase) "a plot of the big interests."[5] The basis for the war was industrial greed and mass deception: it had been made possible (as another character says) only by "oceans of lies" that had deceived "honest, liberal, kindly people."[6] These people, the common people, were deprived of their fundamental liberties not only in the army, but worse, in a "counter-revolutionary" movement taking place in postwar America. Concerted attacks against labor (the lynching of Wobblies and the shooting down of strikers), race riots, Ku Klux Klan raids, and governmentally instituted anti-Bolshevist purges seemed to Dos Passos the overt signs of a deliberate movement to suppress the people while securing the economic supremacy of the big moneyed interests. Perhaps no one incident seemed to him so clearly a violation of America's fundamental ideals as the execution of Sacco and Vanzetti. His character Mary French undoubtedly expresses his own view at the

3. John Dos Passos, "A Preface Twenty-Five Years Later," Preface to *First Encounter* (New York, Philosophical Library, 1945), n.p. *First Encounter* was published originally in 1920 as *One Man's Initiation—1917* (London, George Allen and Unwin, Ltd.).

4. *Ibid.*

5. John Dos Passos, "The 42nd Parallel," *U.S.A.* (New York, Harcourt, Brace and Company, 1938), 412.

6. *One Man's Initiation—1917*, 25.

time of the trials when she says, "If the state of Massachusetts can kill these two innocent men in the face of the protest of the whole world it'll mean that there never will be any justice in America ever again." [7] In his essay "The Wrong Set of Words" he notes that during demonstrations against the Sacco-Vanzetti trials people were being "arrested for distributing the Declaration of Independence." [8] He saw a significant relationship between the war and the execution. The war had "exalted hatred to a virtue"; after the war, the persecution of anarchists and foreigners offered a means for people to release their "pentup hatred and suspicion." [9] His bitterness against the "rightthinking Puritan born Americans" who wanted these men to die arose not only out of his sense of immediate injustice: it grew out of his vision of a past when America had been heroic—at Lexington, Bunker Hill, and Gettysburg—in a continuous historical struggle for human liberty.

Thus, theory and observation directed Dos Passos to the fact of social change. The Marxian dynamic view of history and the actual signs of evolution, revolution, and counter-revolution gave him the sense that these were critical times. For America, repudiating through violence and injustice its democratic ideals, it was indeed a "tragic moment." In a letter to F. Scott Fitzgerald, written in 1936, he says, "We're living in one of the damnedest tragic moments in history";[10] and he goes on to tell Fitzgerald that it is his (Fitzgerald's) moral obligation (as well as, presumably, his own) to write "a first rate novel" about the social tragedy of the times. This was the writer's responsibility—to reveal, and exercise moral judgment upon, the social tendencies of his times. "American writers who want to do the most valuable kind of work [he says in another place] will find themselves trying to discover the deep currents of historical change under the surface of opinions, orthodoxies, heresies, gossip

7. "The Big Money," *U.S.A.*, 451.

8. John Dos Passos, *In All Countries* (New York, Harcourt, Brace and Company, 1934), 177.

9. See *Ibid.*, 173–89.

10. John Dos Passos, "A Letter from Dos Passos to Fitzgerald," in F. Scott Fitzgerald, *The Crack-Up* (ed. by Edmund Wilson, New York, New Directions, 1945), 311. The letter is dated 1936.

and journalistic garbage of the day." [11] Again when he speaks of the
need for a revitalized American theatre, he defines the function of
literature, specifically here of the drama, to be that of a "transformer
for the deep high tension currents of history." [12] The relationship of
literature to its historical times is summarized in his praise of Fitzgerald's unfinished novel, *The Last Tycoon*. This he considered a
"good work" because it had the "quality of detaching itself from its
period while embodying its period" [13] and because in it the author
had "managed to establish that unshakable moral attitude towards
the world we live in and towards its temporary standards that is the
basic essential of a powerful work of imagination." [14] In other
words, a good novel objectified and interpreted contemporary life
from a detached or nonpersonal—that is, a historical—point of
view, and at the same time it passed moral judgment upon the social
life it depicted. Underlying this concept of the novel was a conviction in the power of art to influence the pattern of social change.
"Important" and "compelling" works of art, Dos Passos believed,
could affect the course of social history, for they could "mold and
influence ways of thinking to the point of changing and rebuilding
. . . the mind of the group." [15] Thus, as the serious novelist helped
shape contemporary opinion, he became in effect an "architect of
history." [16]

Technique as Social Commentary in Manhattan Transfer

It is as an architect of history that Dos Passos wrote *Manhattan
Transfer* and *U.S.A.* Both novels dramatize a process of social
change. Their implicit intention is to press upon the public mind
an awareness of a historical drift away from the American ideals of

11. John Dos Passos, "The Writer as Technician," *American Writers' Congress*
(ed. by Henry Hart, New York, International Publishers, 1935), 82.
    12. Dos Passos, "Why Write for the Theatre Anyway?" *Three Plays*, xxii.
    13. Dos Passos, "A Note on Fitzgerald," in Fitzgerald, *The Crack-Up*, 343.
    14. *Ibid.*, 339.
    15. "The Writer as Technician," *American Writers' Congress*, 79.
    16. John Dos Passos, Introduction, *Three Soldiers* (New York, Modern Library,
1932), viii. *Three Soldiers* was published originally in 1921.

democracy, individuality, and liberty. This intention explains the scope and fluidity of these novels, the necessity of showing the passage of years, and of re-creating the essential, if not the total, features of society. While these so-called "collectivist" novels have been criticized by such discerning readers as Malcolm Cowley and Edmund Wilson[17] for not giving full representation to all aspects of American life, to the moral and beautiful as well as the demoralized and sordid, the relevant question is not whether they "tell the whole truth" (to use Delmore Schwartz's phrase[18]): it is whether they discern essential and underlying historical movements. In focusing upon the historical direction of American life, Dos Passos necessarily *abstracted* elements from the American scene. He wanted to show the drift towards monopoly capitalism, and his intention committed him to exclusion as much as to inclusion.

The technical problem inherent in Dos Passos' subject was to find a formal framework to express an interpretation and a moral judgment of the times. His own concept of the novel as a work that detaches itself from the historical period and embodies it committed him to an art of implication. He could not state his judgment of the times explicitly: it had to be inherent in the picture of the times. Moreover, his technique for creating the essential characteristics of the present as a historical period had also to evoke a picture of the past; historical change could be assessed only if the past stood forward as an emotional and social point of reference.

Dos Passos' early novels, *One Man's Initiation, Three Soldiers,* and *Streets of Night,* reveal him groping for a technique. These are the novels of his apprenticeship, and he was not entirely successful in them. With extreme virtuosity, he transformed each impression of the outer world into an aesthetic experience; each slight move-

---

17. See Malcolm Cowley, "Dos Passos: Poet Against the World," *After the Genteel Tradition* (ed. by Malcolm Cowley, New York, Norton and Company, 1937), 168–85; Edmund Wilson, "Dos Passos and the Social Revolution," *New Republic,* Vol. LVIII (April 17, 1929, 256–59; and Joseph Warren Beach, *American Fiction: 1920–1940* (New York, The Macmillan Company, 1941), 41. [For the opinions of Cowley and Wilson see pp. 76 and 31 of this volume.]

18. See Delmore Schwartz, "John Dos Passos and the Whole Truth," *Southern Review,* Vol. IV (Autumn, 1938), 351–67.

ment (for example, the pouring of wine into a glass) into a perfect moment of harmoniously balanced shape and color; each feeling into a dramatic awareness. But meanwhile the total structure of his novel, which was to be the form that would "set the mind of tomorrow's generation," [19] fell apart. Consequently, *One Man's Initiation* displays Dos Passos' craftsmanship in striking imagery, but the social theme is expressed through the device of the apprentice, exposition. Martin Howe must make an explicit condemnation of the war, for neither his view nor the moral attitude of the individualist, the Catholic, the Communist, and the Anarchist is dramatized—they are all flatly stated. *Three Soldiers* evidently had an elaborate aesthetic plan (indicated in the symbolism of the chapter headings), but it broke down as John Andrews, the only character through whose sensibility the outer world took on aesthetic meaning, and the only one who could verbalize a moral attitude towards war, became Dos Passos' direct spokesman. In *Streets of Night,* as in the two earlier novels, the theme of cultural disintegration is expressed through a contrast between the present and the golden past of the Renaissance. But again the theme is developed mainly through direct statement rather than dramatic action; and again Dos Passos is the meticulous master of aesthetic detail. Individual images are arresting but unintegrated with the underlying social theme. The fact that the characters are always talking about their inner sterility may be considered a dramatic device for expressing a view of modern life; more likely it reflects, like the intrusive lush imagery, a failure to make form itself a statement of meaning.

Because these early novels achieved startling aesthetic effects with imagery and because they recalled a romantic past as a judgment upon the present, critics have said that the predominant strain in the early Dos Passos is aesthetic escapism. Malcolm Cowley was the first to suggest that Dos Passos began his career as a "late-Romantic, a tender individualist, an aesthete traveling about the world in an ivory tower" and that he later developed into a "hard-minded real-

19. Dos Passos, Introduction, *Three Soldiers,* viii.

ist, a collectivist, a radical historian of the class struggle." [20] But while Cowley cautioned against drawing too fine a distinction between romantic and realistic strains in Dos Passos, later critics have insisted upon an apparently clear-cut discontinuity between Dos Passos the aesthete and the realist. Yet the novels leading up to *Manhattan Transfer* were already thematically concerned with immediate problems of the times, even if they were not completely successful in finding a formal framework to dramatize the times. Their aestheticism exists superficially in manner, rather than inherently in material. The key scene in *One Man's Initiation,* for example, is that in which the soldiers realistically face the present and discuss possible moral attitudes towards the war as well as plans for social action after the war. In *Three Soldiers,* John Andrews deserts the army in "a gesture" for individual freedom, just as in *Streets of Night,* Wenny chooses suicide as an act of social condemnation. But it is in *Manhattan Transfer* that Dos Passos the "hard-headed realist . . . radical historian of the class struggle" most clearly expresses himself—not because he has arrived at a new realistic stand as a novelist, but because he has achieved, through his apprenticeship, a firmer grasp of his art. *Manhattan Transfer* establishes Dos Passos' control over the techniques of implicatory statement. Here he finally avoids the structural division between dramatic action and expository statement, which in his earlier novels had left his theme unincorporated in form. Here theme and form become an aesthetic integer. The techniques that create the dramatic world of the novel establish toward it a firm social and moral attitude. Thus technique becomes the vehicle of social commentary. The stream of modern history is captured in the novel's dramatic action, structure, pace, mood, symbols, and characters. And as these formal elements create a dramatic world in the dynamic process of social change, they implicitly judge and condemn the historical tendencies of the times.

Since technique is clearly Dos Passos' means of statement, analysis of his technique reveals his social and moral interpretations of city

20. Cowley, "Dos Passos: Poet Against the World," *After the Genteel Tradition,* 168.

life. His is a technique of abstraction which proceeds through an impressionistic method. The result of his technique is not a realistic scene or character in the sense that Dreiser's hotel lobby or restaurant—or a character like Drouet, so consciously modelled after a flesh and blood type—was real. Dos Passos' realism consists in striking essential details abstracted from their total context. Whereas Dreiser accumulates details in order to reproduce the actuality as closely as possible, Dos Passos selects a few evocative details that are to suggest the essential quality of the whole. Thus his realism involves a considerable distortion of actuality, but it is a realism to which the imagination can give assent. If a restaurant is not merely a succession of odors or an East Side street is not merely a succession of colors (of glaring sunlight, patch quilts hanging on fire escapes, pushcarts of fruit), the total scene is suggested by these abstract sensory appeals. Dos Passos' method, then, is to give an impression of reality, rather than to give, like Dreiser, a total cataloguing of actual details. The method of abstraction is fundamental to his creation of the city as a place, an atmosphere, a way of life, and a historical expression of the times. It is fundamental too to his creation of character and of social relationships. The selective process is severely imposed upon all the material of urban life—necessarily so, not only because he was giving a synoptic view of the city (embracing its variety and complexity) but even more important, because he was giving an interpretation of an underlying historical trend. Thus his cityscapes are only fleeting sensuous impressions of scene. His people are only representatives of a human state of mind intrinsic to the city—they are not fully realized flesh and blood people, but abstract states of being. And his total city is not a faithful reproduction of complementary and balancing details: it is an expression of a historical trend. Twentieth-century Manhattan, as Dos Passos portrays it in an abstract literary picture, embodies the trend away from formulated American ideals of a social system that would allow the individual fullest opportunity for equality and personal self-fulfillment as a human being. It symbolizes rather the trend towards a mechanized kind of life that is expressed, in economic terms, in monopoly capitalism, and, in human terms, in the loss of man's human capacities for love and self-realization. The abstract qualities that are presented as urban scenes, characters, atmosphere, social patterns, and historical tendencies are implicit commentaries upon the moral significance of modern American city life. Dos Passos' judgment is inherent in his selective process and in the results of this selective process as a unique and personally envisioned city emerges in the novel as twentieth-century Manhattan.

The brilliant and changing cityscapes are made immediate in brief sensuous impressions, each evocative and incisive, and each giving way to the next in syncopated cinematic movement. As the smallest unit of structure, the fleeting aesthetic impression is ideally suited to the synoptic form, for while it allows for range and flexibility, the rapid transition from one impression to another accelerates the novel's pace to suggest the incessant restless movement within the city itself. The peculiar beauty of the urban scene is created primarily through abstract and kinetic color arrangements. An East Side street, for example, is created as a patterned succession of colors—"a sunstriped tunnel hung with skyblue and smoked-salmon and mustardyellow quilts littered with second hand ginger-bread-colored furniture." [21] On the first page of his first novel, Dos Passos had used the technique of dramatizing color, that is, of giving it the quality of movement, so that abstracted colors "agitate," "flutter," and "slide together." In *Manhattan Transfer,* static scenes become dynamic relationships of color and of light and shadow. Here, for example, in an impression of the Mall at Central Park, colors move and exert pressure: "great rosy and purple and pistachiogreen bubbles of twilight . . . *swell out* of the grass and trees and ponds, *bulge* against the tall houses sharp gray as dead teeth *round* the southern end of the park, *melt* into the indigo zenith." [22] The epigraph on dusk devolving on the city illustrates too that Dos Passos was treating light and shadow, as well as color, as a painter would. Houses, objects, signs, and people appear as chunks of brilliance or shadow, and again the visual appeal is translated into tactile sensations of pressure and into kinetic qualities of movement:

21. Dos Passos, *Manhattan Transfer,* 10.
22. *Ibid.,* 202.

Dusk gently smooths crispangled streets. Dark presses tight the
steaming asphalt city, crushes the fretwork of windows and lettered
signs and chimneys and watertanks and ventilators and fire-escapes
and moldings and patterns and corrugations and eyes and hands and
neckties into blue chunks, into black enormous blocks. Under the
rolling heavier heavier pressure windows blurt light. Night crushes
bright milk out of arclights, squeezes the sullen blocks until they drip
red, yellow, green into streets resounding with feet. All the asphalt
oozes light. Light spurts from lettering on roofs, mills dizzily among
wheels, stains rolling tons of sky.[23]

The beauty of the city lies in its color formations, sometimes brilliant and gaudy, sometimes muted and subdued. All other sensory
details, those of sound, weather, and odor, are oppressively ugly.
The cacophony of the city streets swells from a jumbling of incessant noises—the "growing rumble of traffic," "the frenzied bell of
a fire engine," "the long moan of a steamboat whistle," and the
"children's voices screeching." The people "grope continually
through a tangle of gritty sawedged brittle noise." [24] Grit is palpable
on their lips.[25] The weather oppresses them: in winter a "razor
wind" cuts the ear and makes the forehead ache;[26] in summer a hot
afternoon sun lies on the back like a heavy hand, and "sunlight
squirms in bright worms of heat on [one's] face and hands." [27]

Most offensive of all, and perhaps most brilliantly used for thematic implications, are the odors of New York. A stench seems to rise
from the massing humanity herded in tenements or crowded in
"pigeonhole rooms," "jiggling subways," and jammed busses. Beneath the "goldplated exterior" of the city lies the brutal fact of
man's indignity in a crowded, sweaty world where there is no room.
Ellen's momentary awareness of the "unwashed smell" of a man's
body evokes an image of closeness and fetor: "Under all the nickle-
plated, goldplated streets enameled with May, uneasily she could

23. *Ibid.*, 112.
24. *Ibid.*, 136.
25. *Ibid.*, 263, 266.
26. *Ibid.*, 344.
27. *Ibid.*, 177.

feel the huddling smell, spreading in dark slow crouching masses like corruption oozing from broken sewers." [28] To Jimmy the smell suggests the mass frustration in the city, the "huddling stuffiness of pigeonhole rooms where men and women's bodies writhed alone tortured by the night and the young summer." [29]

From such sharp and kaleidoscopic sensuous impressions of urban scenes, the city is registered immediately in its color, odor, din, and gaudy brilliance. And as it comes to life, it is its own indictment. Under its changing and variegated aspects is the unchanging fact of its oppressiveness: it is a world that grates the nerves and assails the senses with ugliness, clatter, and stench. While these sensuous impressions record the outer scene from the point of view of a disengaged but sensitive observer (Dos Passos himself), the scene is also registered specifically through the eyes of the characters. As they move through the city they perceive people and objects as dissociated images—that is, they do not receive unified and total impressions of entities but only fragmentary impressions of parts of the whole. From a bus, a character sees the street as a succession of "sunshades, summer dresses, straw hats";[30] in the subway he sees people as "elbows, packages, shoulders, buttocks" [31] or as "faces, hats, hands, newspapers jiggling like corn in a popper";[32] and in the street he sees children as "dirty torn shirts, slobbering mouths." [33]

In *Streets of Night,* the dissociated image had been mainly ornamental, expressing Dos Passos' own pleasure in aesthetic moments, rather than related intrinsically to the material of the novel. For example, a series of startling images suggest the impressions received by the three main characters as they walk the streets; but these impressions do not contribute to any larger formal purpose within the novel. Here is sheer indulgence in metaphor by a young writer delighting in his virtuosity:

28. *Ibid.,* 395.
29. *Ibid.,* 194.
30. *Ibid.,* 136.
31. *Ibid.,* 148.
32. *Ibid.,* 356.
33. *Ibid.,* 241.

Faces bloomed and faded through a jumbled luminous mist, white
as plaster casts, red as raw steak, yellow and warted like summer
squashes, smooth and expressionless like cantaloupes. Occasionally a
door yawned black and real in the spinning flicker of the snow and
the lights, or a wall seemed to bulge to splitting with its denseness.[34]

In *Manhattan Transfer,* the dissociated image has integral thematic significance. As it hastens the pace of the novel, it contributes
to the evocation of urban moods and rhythms. As it makes constant
reference to the external scene (even when character or action is mo-
mentarily the center of interest), it underscores the synoptic intention to create the city as protagonist. Most important, as it records
objects of perception as the characters experience them, it implies
a certain quality in the relationship between the character and
other people about him. For example, as Ellen walks along with
Stan, her *manner* of seeing, as reflected in the dissociated image, is
quite different from, say, Carrie's small-town kind of reaction in
Sister Carrie. Carrie responds to people as human beings; one reason
she so deeply envies the well-dressed strangers about her is that she
perceives them as individuals. Ellen, however, sees people in the
same impersonal way she sees objects: "Aloof, as if looking through
thick glass into an aquarium, she watched faces, fruit in storewin-
dows, cans of vegetables, jars of olives, redhotpokerplants . . . newspapers, electric signs . . . sudden jetbright glances of eyes under
straw hats, attitudes of chins, thin lips pouting lips, Cupid's bows,
hungry shadows under cheekbones." [35]

The fact that one's perception of people is on the same level as
the perception of things suggests not only the impersonality in the
city's crowds but also the loneliness within the crowd. In the last
scene of *Manhattan Transfer,* as Jimmy Herf wanders through the
city streets, he too catches dissociated glimpses of faces and disjointed sounds of human footsteps and conversation; but he knows
himself to be essentially alone. In a mood of alienation and loneli-

34. John Dos Passos, *Streets of Night* (New York, George Doran Company, 1923),
192f.
35. *Manhattan Transfer,* 153.

ness, he realizes the barriers of indifference and impersonality that keep people apart—and this forlorn realization contributes to his decision to leave the city.

Just as the external scene is created and assessed by a selective method of impressionism, so is urban time. Time in the sense of tempo runs at the same hectic pace in the personal lives of the characters as in the separate life of the city as a social entity. The quick jagged transition from impression to impression sets the tempo to a rapid nervous beat. As odd moments in the lives of the characters receive stress and time intervals are chosen in an irregular pattern, the movement within the novel becomes syncopated; the novel beats with a jazz tempo that epitomizes the hectic, brassy quality of modern city life. In the same way that Dos Passos had handled color like a painter, he handles variations in time like a jazz musician.

Time in another sense, as crucial moments and as spanning years, is distinct for the characters and for the city. In Jimmy Herf's personal history, the moment when he marries Ellen may be crucial, but in the history of twentieth–century Manhattan this moment is inconsequential. What is important in time for the city is historical sweep that reveals social tendencies. The novel shows Manhattan changing through the decades from an ideal of a modern metropolis (that moves Ed Thatcher and the architects Specker and Sandbourne to a glorious vision of the future) to a disordered world of vice and destruction that sets the mad tramp raving at the end of the novel with a vision of urban doom.

The consequences of the passage of chronological time are revealed in the structure of the novel, which in its circular movement —in the return at the end to the very point of the beginning— expresses the futility of the years. As a unifying element within the synoptic novel, this circular structure imposes a formal pattern, as well as a thematic significance on the numerous and apparently unrelated and inconsequential incidents in the novel. The ferry slip, described in the opening epigraph, is the defining point in the circular movement: at the beginning of the novel it is a place of entry

into the city, and at the end, as Jimmy repudiates New York, it becomes a place of departure. Chapter I develops the theme of coming
to the city by showing the various ways people arrive at New York.
(Ellen is born into urban life; Bud Korpenning migrates from upstate country; and the anonymous Jew of the last scene has immi-
grated.) Once people have found their way into Manhattan, they
are absorbed into its whirling life. The action of the novel moves
them away from the ferry slip towards "the center of things," while a
counteraction directs Jimmy gradually but with growing impetus
back to the ferry slip as a point of escape. Encompassed within the
movement away from and back to the original defining point is the
ironic pattern of action without progress. Action is ceaseless: the
people engage in frenetic affairs of love, business, marriage, and careers; the seasons change; the years pass—but in the end, actions
have cancelled each other, decisions have remained abortive and
plans inchoate, and time has defeated one's hopes in the city. Whatever progress certain characters may seem to have made is more apparent than real. Congo Jake has been transformed from a raga-
muffin to Armand Duval, millionaire bootlegger, but he faces jail;[36]
George Baldwin seems to have achieved success, but his final position is precarious, his inner life void, and his future with Ellen (who
has become emptied of feeling and hopeless) is inauspicious.

The imagery and mood in which entry to the city is expressed
already foreshadow the ugly futility that each character is to face.
Although in the first chapter, the people are yet untouched by city
life, they are described in disagreeable or derogatory images. In the
opening epigraph, the crowds flocking through the ferry slip into
Manhattan are described as pressing "through the manuresmelling
wooden tunnel of the ferryhouse, crushed and jostling like apples
fed down a chute into a press." [37] The newborn baby Ellen is "a
knot of earthworms" squirming in a basket which the nurse holds
away from herself, as though it were a "bedpan"; "the nurse, holding the basket . . . as if it were a bedpan, opened the door to a big
hot dry room with greenish distempered walls where in the air tinc-

36. *Ibid.,* 382.
37. *Ibid.,* 3.

tured with smells of alcohol and iodoform hung writhing a faint sourish squalling from other baskets. . . ." [38]

After this squeamish and offensive picture of birth comes the derogatory image of the country boy's entry. Bud Korpenning is a caricature of the bumpkin: he has red wrists "that stuck out from the frayed sleeves of his coat," a "skinny turkey's throat," blistered "roadswelled feet," sweated temples, and of course, a stock naïve manner.[39] In the last scene of the chapter, the immigrant Jew, inspired by the billboard American, shaves off his beard in a gesture of assimilation. Though the scene is short, the ugliness of New York's East Side is made prominent in the "annihilating clatter of the L trains" and the "rancid sweet huddled smell of packed tenements." [40] Thus, the introductory imagery establishes an attitude towards Manhattan and a prevailing mood that is to function as a unifying element in the novel.

The circular movement into, within, and away from the city is broken into three sections, each of which ends climactically with an act of moral defeat. Section I closes with Bud's suicide after he has failed to get "into the center of things." His melodramatic end adumbrates in a small way the larger pattern of failure in which all of the characters are involved. Except for the fact that his dead body annoys the captain near whose boat it falls, his death passes unnoticed; and even the one reaction of annoyance has thematic implications, for it shows to what extent the nexus of human sympathy has been broken by the urgencies and methods of city life. Bud's failure to make any warm human contacts in the city, his constant sense of aloneness, and his unmourned solitary death are part of, and intrinsic to, the larger pattern of impersonal relationships that exists in the great city. An indifferent world remains unmoved by either his struggles to live or his bitter decision to die.

Section II ends with Ellen's abortion, also an act of death and defeat. Her earlier impulse to bear Stan's child is swept away in the frenetic but sterile activities that make up her life. By this act of

38. *Ibid.*
39. *Ibid.*, 4.
40. *Ibid.*, 10.

abortion she embraces sterility as her destiny. Abortion is symbolic
of an inner emptiness, a loss of humanity, as the normal cycle of
human life is shattered within an encompassing cycle of modern
city life which robs woman of her womanhood and man of his purpose.

Section III ends with Jimmy Herf's indecisive recognition of
this destructive effect of city life. He knows that he must escape from
Manhattan, but this is a negative kind of knowledge, for he does
not know where he must go nor what destiny he must or can create.
The development of his pattern of rejection is the one progressive
movement within the circle of futile and self-vitiating acts. As he
rejects the business world and its goal of success, the impassioned
but futile world of Greenwich Village (inhabited by radicals too far
lost in an alcoholic haze and too deeply demoralized to act), and
finally the entire urban world of overpowering, jutting skyscrapers,
he feels his accomplishment to be that he is at least "beginning to
learn a few of the things I dont want." [41]

41. *Ibid.,* 360.

Manhattan Transfer: Dos Passos' Wasteland

by E. D. Lowry

It goes without saying that the impact of *The Waste Land* on twentieth-century writing has been enormous. Eliot's influence is clearly evinced in much of the poetry produced since 1922 and can even be detected in such prose masterpieces of the Lost Generation as *The Great Gatsby* and *The Sun Also Rises*. Critics have, however, hitherto overlooked John Dos Passos' heavy debt to the poet in *Manhattan Transfer* (1925), a novel conceived and published when the stir created by *The Waste Land* was at its height. An exploration of the affinities between the two works may not only be worth while in itself, but, more important, may help us estimate more accurately the significance of Dos Passos' novel and the special quality of his vision.

Perhaps the most obvious similarity between *The Waste Land* and *Manhattan Transfer* is their use of the structural principle of dissociation and recombination. Like Eliot, Dos Passos disintegrates the usual discursive ordering of experience so as to bring together apparently unrelated fragments of actuality which, seen in juxtaposition, coalesce into a new unity expressing a "total" view of his subject. The two writers, coming to grips with the clashing contradictions and chaotic quality of modern life, capitalize to the utmost on the possibilities of shock effect, discord, discontinuity. Just as one vignette in *The Waste Land* melts without warning or transition into the next, so too in *Manhattan Transfer* scene follows scene abruptly, each dissolving unexpectedly into another, the chief unify-

"*Manhattan Transfer*: Dos Passos' Wasteland" by E. D. Lowry. From *The University Review* (1963), pp. 47–52. Reprinted by permission of the author and of *New Letters,* copyright holder for The University Review (University of Missouri).

ing factor being the thematic device of "the city" and the spiritual atmosphere associated with it.

However, as scholars have generally realized, the seemingly disjunct components of *The Waste Land* are arranged in such a way as to comment upon each other; they are in one sense "different," in another "the same." This also holds true for Dos Passos' book. In one section of the novel, for instance, Ellen Thatcher is glimpsed on her honeymoon trip with Jojo Oglethorpe, a crucial event in her life; the following episode, in which Jimmy Herf turns down the possibility of a prosperous career in Uncle Jeff's firm, is superficially different yet actually similar in that it too brings to light the notion of a decisive turning-point in a character's life.[1] Of much greater significance, however, is the contrast in the attitudes of Ellen and Jimmy: Ellen, through an opportunistic marriage to the degenerate Oglethorpe, prostitutes herself for the sake of material success, a value which Herf firmly renounces when he thinks to himself that "Uncle Jeff and his office can go plumb to hell" (p. 121). Instances of this sort abound in *Manhattan Transfer* and it would profit little to multiply examples; suffice it to say that the dissociated elements of Dos Passos' novel are just as meaningfully ordered by a complex pattern of thematic correspondences and dissimilarities as the parts of *The Waste Land*.

Another factor lending cohesion to the apparently discordant texture of their work is the conviction, on the part of both writers, that modern urban-industrial life is synonymous with futility, spiritual stagnation, nothingness. This concept arises not so much from a notation of the outer aspects of the world they study as from an effort to convey the "feel" of its inner significance. The "content" of *Manhattan Transfer,* as of *The Waste Land,* is to a substantial degree something which is felt rather than stated: an overriding sense of moral impoverishment generated in great measure by a careful choice of imagery. And time after time the quality of Dos Passos' imagery puts the reader in mind of *The Waste Land,* with its "mud-

1. *Manhattan Transfer* (New York, 1925), pp. 115–121. Parenthetical page numbers in my text refer to this work and edition.

cracked houses," "dirty ears," and "bats with baby faces." [2] At the very outset of the novel, the "broken boxes, orange-rinds, spoiled cabbage heads" floating in the ferry slip (p. 3) set the mood for what is to come and—like the "empty bottles, sandwich papers, Silk handkerchiefs, cardboard boxes cigarette ends" customarily littering Eliot's Thames (ll. 177–178)—characterize an entire culture.

The emotional key struck by these initial images is sustained throughout the rest of *Manhattan Transfer*. Over a store selling out is a sign reading "WE HAVE MADE A TERRIBLE MISTAKE" (p. 144). On a stoop an old man sobs: "Don't you see I cant . . . ? I cant . . . I cant" (p. 376). Joe Harland looks out at "a piece of the dun wall of an air-shaft and a man with a green eye-shade staring vacantly out of a window" (p. 144). A similar impression of impotence and aimlessness emerges from the burglar alarm that rings all night, tormenting Jimmy (p. 173); and from the phonograph record that goes on "rasping round and round" as Stan and Ellen make love (p. 216). If Eliot's Fisher King beholds a procession of the dead crossing London Bridge, Dos Passos offers much the same spectacle when a subway car becomes for Ruth Prynne "A trainload of jiggling corpses, nodding and swaying . . ." (pp. 293–294). The life that Jimmy rejects by leaving the city—with its "desert backyards" (p. 186) and "desolate empty pavements" (p. 154)—is manifested on the last page by his passing, on the New Jersey shore, "dumping grounds full of smoking rubbish-piles," "shapeless masses of corroding metal" (p. 404). Using symbolism and imagery to project a mood, Dos Passos, like Eliot, supplants discursive unity by a unity of feeling which at the same time conveys his attitude toward the theme.

The insight which underlies a symbolism of aridity and impotence in both *The Waste Land* and *Manhattan Transfer* is reducible to the conviction that modern man has died an emotional death, his potentialities for true affective response drained away by a dehumanized social order. This crisis in man's instinctive life—high-

---

2. *The Waste Land* (New York, 1922), ll. 345, 103, 379. Parenthetical line numbers in my text refer to this work and edition.

lighted by Eliot's image of the listless typist who, after the departure
of her lover, "smoothes her hair with automatic hand, / And puts a
record on the gramophone" (ll. 255–256)—is the problem to which
Dos Passos turns on virtually every page of his novel. Billy Wal-
dron's seemingly innocent remark about conditions in the theater—
"Oh I know everything is dead" (p. 292)—sums up the bearing of
Manhattan Transfer as a whole. "Broken doll[s] in the ranks of var-
nished articulated dolls . . ." (p. 249), sapped of vitality, sponta-
neity, and a capacity for joy, the plight of most of Dos Passos' characters tends to resemble that of the barren Emily Baldwin, "faded
and elegant and biting her lips and . . . hating life" (p. 279). This
basic sterility, this affective numbness, comes to the fore in a number
of ways: in the almost total absence of authentic love throughout
Manhattan Transfer; in the homosexuality of Oglethorpe and Tony
Hunter; in the abortions of Ellen and Cassie Wilkins; in the promis-
cuity of Anna Cohen and Nevada Jones; in the physical devitaliza-
tion of Mrs. Herf and Mrs. Thatcher; and, most strikingly, in the
horrible episode of the abortionist whose activities foul the plumbing of an entire apartment house.

The direction of Dos Passos' thinking in this respect can be more
easily gauged by understanding Ellen's relationship to her successive
lovers in terms of *The Waste Land,* where the regeneration of the
blighted kingdom depended on the successful love-making of the Deliverer and Woman. Ellen represents the ruthlessness, the readiness
to subordinate human values to the exigencies of "success," which
characterize the city as a whole. Although she enjoys being called
"Elaine the lily maid" and "Helena" (pp. 54, 277)—and is thus
placed, like Eliot's Woman, in ironic juxtaposition to beauties of the
past—it is owing to her hard, willful temperament, the absence in
her of the tender qualities associated with women, that she makes
her way to the top on Broadway in *The Zinnia Girl* (p. 243), a possible echo of Eliot's "hyacinth girl" (l. 36). The mistress or wife of
four different men, Ellen nevertheless undergoes a steady dehumani-
zation, grows increasingly frigid and unresponsive, until she is transformed into "a porcelain figure under a bellglass" (p. 300), conscious

only of a "gradual icy coldness stealing through her like novocaine" (p. 375).

The men who in different ways try implicitly to rekindle Ellen's affective powers and thus bring life to the urban wasteland, fail because, like the various "incarnations" of Eliot's Deliverer, their love-making with the Woman (Ellen) is always futile, unproductive, or marred by neurotic pressures. Oglethorpe is sexually perverted; Stan (and this is why Ellen is more strongly attracted to him than the others) is obsessed with death; Baldwin is intent mainly upon money and power. These would-be Deliverers are themselves crippled by the moral and emotional enervation they would relieve; unable or unwilling to direct their masculine energies toward fruitful, life-enhancing ends, they are foredoomed to frustration.

Jimmy alone seems to have a chance. If Ellen is *of* the city and to some extent its symbolic embodiment (the book opens with her birth), Jimmy, though born in New York, comes upon the scene from the outside, returning from Europe on the Fourth of July, a holiday associated with high hopes and new beginnings. But as his character develops, it becomes evident that Jimmy represents the male spirit in the grip of another fatal disability; given to an excessive aestheticism, he is, as C. M. Bowra remarks of a later incarnation of Eliot's Deliverer, "cut off from life and lives among dreams and desires." [3] Herf perceives his plight when he reflects that his work as a reporter has made him "a parasite on the drama of life" and caused him to look at everything "through a peephole" (p. 320). "The trouble with me," he admits, "is I cant decide what I want most, so my motion is circular, helpless and confoundedly discouraging" (p. 176); "I havent even got the conviction to make a successful drunkard" (p. 384).

Turning his back on bourgeois society, giving up his job and drifting about the city, Jimmy exemplifies in his own aimless quest for "something new" (p. 384) the purposelessness of the metropolis he hates. Seeking "refuge in the past," sinking into "dreamier and

---

3. *The Creative Experiment* (New York, 1958), p. 168. I am deeply indebted to Mr. Bowra's discussion of the Deliverer-Woman theme in *The Waste Land*.

dreamier reverie" (p. 322), his failure is ultimately a failure of true male assertiveness and vitality; unable to awaken in Ellen a positive response to life, he is incapable in a larger sense of redeeming the prevailing urban desolation. Although he achieves what looks like a solitary salvation by leaving New York, even this gesture, with its hint of "symbolic suicide," [4] suggests merely another dead end.

Another thematic device linking *Manhattan Transfer* to *The Waste Land* is the use of fire and water symbolism.[5] This symbolic design is clearly indicated by Dos Passos' allusion, in a prose poem dealing with the Great War, to "death in fire, death in water" (p. 271). Bud Korpenning, two nameless highjackers, and Martin Schiff die—or probably die—by drowning (pp. 125, 324, 362). Just before Blackhead expires, his daughter walks in wearing a raincoat and carrying a wet umbrella (p. 393). Water, in the form of snow, counterpoints the successive crises of the Herfs' marriage (pp. 298, 329, 344). As a prelude to his death, Stan is found, on a rainy night (p. 209), floating unconscious in a bathtub (p. 213); and on his last wild escapade he walks the drizzling streets to take a trip on the ferry (p. 250). It is also raining shortly before Bud drowns himself (p. 124), and on the night Mrs. Herf is stricken by a fatal illness (p. 78). During the torrential rain which marks the beginning of her hopeless marriage to Oglethorpe, Ellen is haunted by the song "Long-legged Jack of the Isthmus": "Oh it rained forty days / And it rained forty nights" (p. 118). The tune "One More River to Jordan" is another thematic chord in the book (pp. 250–251, 255). Then, even as Jimmy is about to leave the city for the last time, the death-oriented culture he cannot accept, yet cannot redeem, is materialized in the beckoning figure of a prostitute in a raincoat (p. 402).

Imbued with the same negative, lethal overtones as his water imagery is Dos Passos' fire symbolism. Stan is burned to death in a

---

4. Malcolm Cowley, "Dos Passos: Poet Against the World," in *After the Genteel Tradition,* ed. M. Cowley (New York, 1937), p. 173.

5. Georges-Albert Astre (*Thèmes et structures dans l'oeuvre de John Dos Passos,* I [Paris, 1956], 190) has mentioned the fire and water imagery in *Manhattan Transfer*; however, he does not explore this symbolic structure or connect it with Eliot.

drunken frenzy (p. 253), whereas Anna Cohen is badly disfigured by a blaze at Madame Soubrine's (p. 399). Bud plunges to his death at dawn, when "The windows of Manhattan have caught fire" (p. 125); similarly, "All the windows on the east side of the avenue were aflame" (p. 395) when Ellen turns away from the immigrant boy and the authentic life he seems to represent. The destructive aspects of the city, the anxiety and insecurity which lie beneath its routinized surface, are manifested by a pyromaniac terrorizing New York with his insane handiwork (pp. 14, 115). Susie Thatcher is tormented by thoughts of fire (p. 22), and young Jimmy is frightened when he passes a man he suspects of being the firebug (p. 83). Appearing throughout the novel, usually at significant junctures, is the fateful image of the fire engine. Jimmy, who is to fail as a "Deliverer," sees a fire engine speeding by the day he arrives in the city with his mother (p. 71). The roar of fire apparatus is heard after Stan's narrow escape from drowning (p. 216), in the midst of his death scene (pp. 252–253), when Ellen leaves the abortionist's office (p. 268), and after Schiff's apparent suicide (p. 362).

Even if Ellen hears someone speak of "Fire that purifies" (p. 139), fire alone cannot make barren ground fruitful again. Water, however, can bring life as well as take it away. In a metropolitan desert recalling Eliot's place of "dry sterile thunder without rain" (l. 342), the childless Emily Baldwin, her head aching as though it were bound with "hot wire," looking out her window at a new building rising against a "flame-blue sky," can hear a "low growl of thunder" and see "beyond to the northwest a shining head of clouds . . . blooming compactly like a cauliflower. Oh," she thinks, "if it would only rain" (p. 185). Walking in midsummer heat along the "quivering street" and "melting asphalt," Ellen watches a soaring cumulus and exclaims, "Isnt that a fine cloud? Wouldnt it be fine if we had a rip-roaring thunderstorm?" (p. 200). Later, she thinks of New York, with its "sky of beaten lead that never snows," and asks desperately, "O God why wont it snow?" (p. 262).

The desiccation of modern marriage is suggested by Mrs. Hildebrand's ignorance concerning the availability of milk in New York (p. 278), and by the empty milk bottle outside the Herfs' door (p.

303). When the abortionist clogs the plumbing in Alice Sheffield's apartment house, the episode is rendered doubly meaningful by the fact "There wasnt a drop of water in the house all day yesterday" (p. 378). And, in the final stages of the novel, after Ellen has irrevocably committed herself to the arid ways of the city, she has a vague feeling she has left something behind in a taxi, but she knows it could not have been her umbrella (p. 400), for no life-giving rain—the sort conspicuously absent in *Manhattan Transfer* —will ever freshen her parched existence.

Overarching this vision of a civilization, consumed on the one hand by the fires of lawless passion and suffering on the other from severe spiritual drought, is a consciousness, not unlike that found in *The Waste Land,* of historical parallelism. Eliot's catalog of doomed cities—"Falling towers / Jerusalem Athens Alexandria / Vienna London" (ll. 373–375)—finds its counterpart in the speech of the half-crazed tramp who, standing by a blazing campfire, likens Dos Passos' New York to Babylon and Nineveh and warns of "the fire an brimstone an the earthquake an the tidal wave . . ." (p. 381) which will engulf "the City of Destruction" (p. 366), the "City of orgies walks and joys" (p. 174).

Aside from the obvious value of taking into account a possible literary debt which has previously passed unnoticed, and showing that *Manhattan Transfer* is a richer and more complex book than it is generally thought to be, the end result of the foregoing analysis should be to throw into relief an aspect of the novelist's mind which has not been sufficiently emphasized: the fact that Dos Passos' vision, attuned as it is to the problem of evil, to the forces which can corrupt and contaminate the spiritual texture of life, is perhaps closer to that of Eliot than it is to the outlook of Crane, Dreiser, or Farrell, writers with whom he is frequently bracketed. Although the configurations of visible reality form the springboard for his critique, it is ultimately his obsessive concern with the contours of man's inner world which constitutes the energizing center of his work. Understood in this light, *Manhattan Transfer* is no more "naturalistic" than *The Waste Land.*

John Dos Passos and *1919*

by *Jean-Paul Sartre*

A novel is a mirror. So everyone says. But what is meant by
reading a novel? It means, I think, jumping into the mirror. You
suddenly find yourself on the other side of the glass, among people
and objects that have a familiar look. But they merely look familiar.
We have never really seen them. The things of our world have,
in turn, become outside reflections. You close the book, step over
the edge of the mirror and return to this honest-to-goodness world,
and you find furniture, gardens and people who have nothing to
say to you. The mirror that closed behind you reflects them peace-
fully, and now you would swear that art is a reflection. There are
clever people who go so far as to talk of distorting mirrors.

Dos Passos very consciously uses this absurd and insistent illusion
to impel us to revolt. He had done everything possible to make his
novel seem a mere reflection. He has even donned the garb of
populism. The reason is that his art is not gratuitous; he wants to
prove something. But observe what a curious aim he has. He wants
to show us this world, our own—to *show* it only, without explanations or comment. There are no revelations about the machinations
of the police, the imperialism of the oil kings or the Ku-Klux-Klan,
no cruel pictures of poverty. We have already seen everything he
wants to show us, and, so it seems at first glance, seen it exactly as
he wants us to see it. We recognize immediately the sad abundance
of these untragic lives. They are our own lives, these innumerable,

"John Dos Passos and *1919*." From *Literary and Philosophical Essays by Jean-
Paul Sartre*, translated by Annette Michelson, pp. 88–96. Copyright © 1955 by
Rider & Company, London. Reprinted by permission of Hutchinson Publishing
Group Ltd. (Originally published in *Situations I* by Librairie Gallimard, Paris,
1947.)

planned, botched, immediately forgotten and constantly renewed adventures that slip by without leaving a trace, without involving anyone, until the time when one of them, no different from any of the others, suddenly, as if through some clumsy trickery, sickens a man for good and throws a mechanism out of gear.

Now, it is by depicting, as we ourselves might depict, these too familiar appearances with which we all put up that Dos Passos makes them unbearable. He arouses indignation in people who never get indignant, he frightens people who fear nothing. But hasn't there been some sleight-of-hand? I look about me and see people, cities, boats, the war. But they aren't the real thing; they are discreetly queer and sinister, as in a nightmare. My indignation against this world also seems dubious to me; it only faintly resembles the other indignation, the kind that a mere news item can arouse. I am on the other side of the mirror.

Dos Passos' hate, despair and lofty contempt are real. But that is precisely why his world is not real; it is a created object. I know of none—not even Faulkner's or Kafka's—in which the art is greater or better hidden. I know of none that is more precious, more touching or closer to us. This is because he takes his material from our world. And yet, there is no stranger or more distant world. Dos Passos has invented only one thing, an art of story-telling. But that is enough to create a universe.

We live in time, we calculate in time. The novel, like life, unfolds in the present. The perfect tense exists on the surface only; it must be interpreted as a present *with aesthetic distance,* as a stage device. In the novel the dice are not loaded, for fictional man is free. He develops before our eyes; our impatience, our ignorance, our expectancy are the same as the hero's. The tale, on the other hand, as Fernandez has shown, develops in the past. But the tale explains. Chronological order, life's order, barely conceals the causal order, which is an order for the understanding. The event does not touch us; it stands half-way between fact and law. Dos Passos' time is his own creation; it is neither fictional nor narrative. It is rather, if you like, historical time. The perfect and imperfect tenses are not used simply to observe the rules; the reality of Joe's or of Eveline's adventures lies in the fact they are now part of the past. Every-thing is told as if by someone who is remembering.

> "*The years Dick was little* he never heard anything about his Dad. . . ." "All Eveline thought about *that winter* was going to the Art Institute. . . ." "They waited two weeks in Vigo while the officials quarrelled about their status and they got pretty fed up with it."

The fictional event is a nameless presence; there is nothing one can say about it, for it develops. We may be shown two men comb-ing a city for their mistresses, but we are not told that they "do not find them," for this is not true. So long as there remains one street, one café, one house to explore, it is not yet true. In Dos Passos, the things that happen are named first, and then the dice are cast, as they are in our memories.

> Glen and Joe only got ashore for a few hours and couldn't find Marcelline and Loulou.

The facts are clearly outlined; they are ready for *thinking about.* But Dos Passos never thinks them. Not for an instant does the order of causality betray itself in chronological order. There is no narrative, but rather the jerky unreeling of a rough and uneven memory, which sums up a period of several years in a few words only to dwell languidly over a minute fact. Like our real memories, it is a jumble of miniatures and frescoes. There is relief enough, but it is cunningly scattered at random. One step further would give us the famous idiot's monologue in *The Sound and the Fury.* But that would still involve intellectualizing, suggesting an explana-tion in terms of the irrational, suggesting a Freudian order beneath this disorder. Dos Passos stops just in time. As a result of this, past things retain a flavour of the present; they still remain, in their exile, what they once were, inexplicable tumults of colour, sound and passion. Each event is irreducible, a gleaming and solitary *thing* that does not flow from anything else, but suddenly arises to join other things. For Dos Passos, narrating means adding. This ac-counts for the slack air of his style. "And . . . and . . . and . . ." The great disturbing phenomena—war, love, political movements, strikes—fade and crumble into an infinity of little odds and ends which can just about be set side by side. Here is the armistice:

> In early November rumours of an armistice began to fly around and then suddenly one afternoon Major Wood ran into the office that Eleanor and Eveline shared and dragged them both away from their desks and kissed them both and shouted, "At last it's come." Before she knew it Eveline found herself kissing Major Moorehouse right on the mouth. The Red Cross office turned into a college dormitory the night of a football victory: it was the Armistice.
>
> Everybody seemed suddenly to have bottles of cognac and to be singing, *There's a long trail awinding* or *La Madel-lon pour nous n'est pas sévère.*

These Americans see war the way Fabrizio saw the battle of Waterloo. And the intention, like the method, is clear upon reflection. But you must close the book and reflect.

Passions and gestures are also things. Proust analysed them, related them to former states and thereby made them inevitable. Dos Passos wants to retain only their factual nature. All he is allowed to say is, "In that place and at that time Richard was that way, and at another time, he was different." Love and decisions are great spheres that rotate on their own axes. The most we can grasp is a kind of *conformity* between the psychological state and the exterior situation, something resembling a colour harmony. We may also suspect that explanations are *possible,* but they seem as frivolous and futile as a spider-web on a heavy red flower. Yet, never do we have the feeling of fictional freedom: Dos Passos imposes upon us instead the unpleasant impression of an indeterminacy of detail. Acts, emotions and ideas suddenly settle within a character, make themselves at home and then disappear without his having much to say in the matter. You cannot say he submits to them. He experiences them. There seems to be no law governing their appearance.

Nevertheless, they once did exist. This lawless past is irremediable. Dos Passos has purposely chosen the perspective of history to tell a story. He wants to make us feel that the stakes are down. In *Man's Hope,* Malraux says, more or less, that "the tragic thing about death is that it transforms life into a destiny." With the opening lines of

his book, Dos Passos settles down into death. The lives he tells
about are all closed in on themselves. They resemble those Berg-
sonian memories which, after the body's death, float about, lifeless
and full of odours and lights and cries, through some forgotten
limbo. We constantly have the feeling that these vague, human
lives are destinies. Our own past is not at all like this. There is not
one of our acts whose meaning and value we cannot still transform
even now. But beneath the violent colours of these beautiful,
motley objects that Dos Passos presents there is something petrified.
Their significance is fixed. Close your eyes and try to remember
your own life, try to remember it *that way;* you will stifle. It is this
unrelieved stifling that Dos Passos wanted to express. In capitalist
society, men do not have lives, they have only destinies. He never
says this, but he makes it felt throughout. He expresses it discreetly, cautiously, until we feel like smashing our destinies. We
have become rebels; he has achieved his purpose.

We are rebels *behind the looking-glass.* For that is not what the
rebel of this world wants to change. He wants to transform Man's
present condition, the one that develops day by day. Using the past
tense to tell about the present means using a device, creating a
strange and beautiful world, as frozen as one of those Mardi-Gras
masks that become frightening on the faces of real, living men.

But whose memories are these that unfold through the novel? At
first glance, they seem to be those of the heroes, of Joe, Dick, Fillette
and Eveline. And, on occasion, they are. As a rule, whenever a character is sincere, whenever he is bursting with something, no matter
how, or with what:

> When he went off duty he'd walk home achingly tired through the
> strawberry-scented early Parisian morning, thinking of the faces and
> the eyes and the sweat-drenched hair and the clenched fingers clotted
> with blood and dirt . . .

But the narrator often ceases to coincide completely with the
hero. The hero could not quite have said what he does say, but
you feel a discreet complicity between them. The narrator relates
from the outside what the hero would have wanted him to relate.
By means of this complicity, Dos Passos, without warning us, has

us make the transition he was after. We suddenly find ourselves inside a horrible memory whose every recollection makes us uneasy, a bewildering memory that is no longer that of either the characters or the author. It seems like a chorus that remembers, a sententious chorus that is accessory to the deed.

> All the same he got along very well at school and the teachers liked him, particularly Miss Teazle, the English teacher, because he had nice manners and said little things that weren't fresh but that made them laugh. Miss Teazle said he showed real feeling for English composition. One Christmas he sent her a little rhyme he made up about the Christ Child and the three Kings and she declared he had a gift.

The narration takes on a slightly stilted manner, and everything that is reported about the hero assumes the solemn quality of a public announcement: ". . . she declared he had a gift." The sentence is not accompanied by any comment, but acquires a sort of collective resonance. It is a *declaration.* And indeed, whenever we want to know his characters' thoughts, Dos Passos, with respectful objectivity, generally gives us their declarations.

> Fred . . . said the last night before they left he was going to tear loose. When they got to the front he might get killed and then what? Dick said he liked talking to the girls but that the whole business was too commercial and turned his stomach. Ed Schuyler, who'd been nicknamed Frenchie and was getting very continental in his ways, said that the street girls were too naive.

I open *Paris-Soir* and read, "*From our special correspondent:* Charlie Chaplin declares that he has put an end to Charlie." Now I have it! Dos Passos reports all his characters' utterances to us in the style of a statement to the Press. Their words are thereby cut off from thought, and become pure utterances, simple reactions that must be registered as such, in the behaviourist style upon which Dos Passos draws when it suits him to do so. But, at the same time, the utterance takes on a social importance; it is inviolable, it becomes a maxim. Little does it matter, thinks the satisfied chorus, what Dick had in mind when he spoke that sentence. What matters is that it has been uttered. Besides, it was not formed inside

him, it came from afar. Even before he uttered it, it existed as a
pompous sound, a taboo. All he has done is to lend it his power of
affirmation. It is as if there were a Platonic heaven of words and
commonplaces to which we all go to find words suitable to a given
situation. There is a heaven of gestures, too. Dos Passos makes a
pretence of presenting gestures as pure events, as mere exteriors,
as free, animal movements. But this is only appearance. Actually,
in relating them, he adopts the point of view of the chorus, of
public opinion. There is no single one of Dick's or of Eleanor's
gestures which is not a public demonstration, performed to a hum-
ming accompaniment of flattery.

> At Chantilly they went through the château and fed the big carp in
> the moat. They ate their lunch in the woods, sitting on rubber cush-
> ions. J.W. kept everybody laughing explaining how he hated picnics,
> asking everybody what it was that got into even the most intelligent
> women that they were always trying to make people go on picnics.
> After lunch they drove out to Senlis to see the houses that the Uh-
> lans had destroyed there in the battle of the Marne.

Doesn't it sound like a local newspaper's account of an ex-
servicemen's banquet? All of a sudden, as the gesture dwindles until
it is no more than a thin film, we see that it *counts,* that it is sacred
in character and that, at the same time, it involves commitment. But
for whom? For the abject consciousness of "everyman," for what
Heidegger calls "das Mann." But still, where does it spring from?
Who is its representative as I read? *I* am. In order to understand
the words, in order to make sense out of the paragraphs, I first have
to adopt his point of view. I have to play the role of the obliging
chorus. This consciousness exists only through me; without me
there would be nothing but black spots on white paper. But even
while I *am* this collective consciousness, I want to wrench away
from it, to see it from the judge's point of view, that is, to get free
of myself. This is the source of the shame and uneasiness with which
Dos Passos knows how to fill the reader. I am a reluctant accomplice
(though I am not even sure that I am reluctant), creating and rejecting social taboos. I am, deep in my heart, a revolutionary again, an
unwilling one.

In return, how I hate Dos Passos' men! I am given a fleeting glimpse of their minds, just enough to see that they are living animals. Then, they begin to unwind their endless tissue of ritual statements and sacred gestures. For them, there is no break between inside and outside, between body and consciousness, but only between the stammerings of an individual's timid, intermittent, fumbling thinking and the messy world of collective representations. What a simple process this is, and how effective! All one need do is use American journalistic technique in telling the story of a life, and like the Salzburg reed, a life crystallizes into the Social, and the problem of the transition to the typical—stumbling-block of the social novel—is thereby resolved. There is no further need to present a working man type, to compose (as Nizan does in *Antoine Bloyé*) an existence which represents the exact average of thousands of existences. Dos Passos, on the contrary, can give all his attention to rendering a single life's special character. Each of his characters is unique; what happens to him could happen to no one else. What does it matter, since Society has marked him more deeply than could any special circumstance, since *he is* Society? Thus, we get a glimpse of an order beyond the accidents of fate or the contingency of detail, an order more supple than Zola's physiological necessity or Proust's psychological mechanism, a soft and insinuating constraint which seems to release its victims, letting them go only to take possession of them again without their suspecting, in other words, a statistical determinism. These men, submerged in their own existences, live as they can. They struggle; what comes their way is not determined in advance. And yet, neither their efforts, their faults, nor their most extreme violence can interfere with the regularity of births, marriages and suicides. The pressure exerted by a gas on the walls of its container does not depend upon the individual histories of the molecules composing it.

We are still on the other side of the looking-glass. Yesterday you saw your best friend and expressed to him your passionate hatred of war. Now try to relate this conversation to yourself in the style of Dos Passos. "And they ordered two beers and said that war was hateful. Paul declared he would rather do anything than fight and John said he agreed with him and both got excited and said they were glad they agreed. On his way home, Paul decided to see John more often." You will start hating yourself immediately. It will not take you long, however, to decide that you *cannot* use this tone in talking about yourself. However insincere you may have been, you were at least living out your insincerity, playing it out on your own, continuously creating and extending its existence from one moment to the next. And even if you got caught up in collective representations, you had first to experience them as personal resignation. We are neither mechanical objects nor possessed souls, but something worse; we are free. We exist either entirely *within* or entirely *without*. Dos Passos' man is a hybrid creature, an interior-exterior being. We go on living with him and within him, with his vacillating, individual consciousness, when suddenly it wavers, weakens, and is diluted in the collective consciousness. We follow it up to that point and suddenly, before we notice, we are on the outside. The man behind the looking–glass is a strange, contemptible, fascinating creature. Dos Passos knows how to use this constant shifting to fine effect. I know of nothing more gripping than Joe's death.

> Joe laid out a couple of frogs and was backing off towards the door, when he saw in the mirror that a big guy in a blouse was bringing down a bottle on his head held with both hands. He tried to swing around but he didn't have time. The bottle crashed his skull and he was out.

We are inside with him, until the shock of the bottle on his skull. Then immediately, we find ourselves outside with the chorus, part of the collective memory, ". . . and he was out." Nothing gives you a clearer feeling of annihilation. And from then on, each page we turn, each page that tells of other minds and of a world going on without Joe, is like a spadeful of earth over our bodies. But it is a behind-the-looking-glass death: all we really get is the fine *appearance* of nothingness. True nothingness can neither be felt nor thought. Neither you nor I, nor anyone after us, will ever have anything to say about our real deaths.

Dos Passos' world—like those of Faulkner, Kafka and Stendhal—is impossible because it is contradictory. But therein lies its beauty. Beauty is a veiled contradiction. I regard Dos Passos as the greatest writer of our time.

A Serious Artist

by F. R. Leavis

After *Manhattan Transfer* (1927) one remembered the name of John Dos Passos. After *The Forty-second Parallel* one looked eagerly forward to the succeeding members of the trilogy (for something of that order seemed to be promised) in the conviction that we had here a work demanding serious attention as no other appearing under the head of the novel during the past two or three years had done. *Nineteen-nineteen* is a challenge to justify the conviction.

The Forty-second Parallel established Mr. Dos Passos as an unusually serious artist—serious with the seriousness that expresses itself in the propagandist spirit. Unlike Mrs. Woolf, his antithesis, he cannot be interested in individuals without consciously relating them to the society and the civilization that make the individual life possible. Consequently, society and civilization being to-day what they are, his stress falls elsewhere than upon the individual life as such. In *Manhattan Transfer* his theme is New York, representing our "megalopolitan" civilization: "The terrible thing about having New York go stale on you is that there's nowhere else. It's the top of the world. All we can do is to go round and round in a squirrel's cage."

The undertaking involves a peculiar technical problem, one that none of the methods customarily associated with the novel will meet. No amount of enthusiasm for collective humanity will dispose of the fact that it is only in individuals that humanity lives, that only in the individual focus does consciousness function, that

"A Serious Artist" by F. R. Leavis. From *Scrutiny* (1932), pp 173–79. Reprinted by permission of the publisher, Cambridge University Press.

only individuals enjoy and suffer; and the problem is to suggest the multitudinous impersonality of the ant-heap through individual cases that, without much development, interest us as such. *Manhattan Transfer* represents a sufficient degree of success. It is of the essence of Mr. Dos Passos' method here—and of his vision of modern life—that of no one of his swirl of "cases" do we feel that it might profitably be developed into a separate novel; and yet we are interested enough. Here we have them in poignant individuality, a representative assortment of average men and women, engaged in the "pursuit of happiness"—a pursuit sanctioned by the Constitution, but, of its very nature, and by the very conditions of the civilization to which they belong, vain. "Darling, I'm so happy. . . . It's really going to be worth living now." Money, Success, Security, Love—in varied and ironical iteration we see the confident clutch: " 'Elaine,' he said shakily, 'life's really going to mean something to me now. . . . God, if you knew how empty life had been for so many years. I've been like a tin mechanical toy, all hollow inside.' "

Manhattan Transfer ends with Jimmy Herf (the character to whom the author seems closest) walking, with an air of symbolic finality, out of New York. *The Forty-second Parallel* gives us the America into which he walks—a large undertaking, which calls for some modification of technique. The representative lives stand out more and are given less in episode-dialogue and more in consecutive narrative; narrative admirably managed in *tempo*, and varied dramatically in idiom with the chief actor. The "Newsreels" interspersed at intervals are a new device, their function being by means of newspaper-clippings and the like, in ironical medley, to establish the background of the contemporary public world. Moreover, also at intervals, there are lives, admirably compressed and stylized in what might be called prose-poems, of the makers, the heroes, the great men, the public figures, of American civilization. Thus Mr. Dos Passos seeks to provide something corresponding to the symbolic figures of a national epic or saga.

In general, for him, to be representative is to be unimpressive, and of his private characters only one is impressive and saga-like in

his representativeness: J. Ward Moorhouse, "public relations counsel." It is significant. In him is embodied the power that, in the
general disintegration, in the default of religion, art and traditional
forms and sanctions, holds society together—the Power of the Word,
or, let us say, Advertising. "Clean cut young executive," says J. Ward
Moorhouse, looking at himself in the glass: the magician has reason
to believe in the magic; it works for him. On this theme the author's
art achieves some of its triumphs, and the aspect of modern civilization it exhibits is terrifying. "We are handling this matter from the
human interest angle . . . . pity and tears, you understand"—can
a hundred D. H. Lawrences preserve even the idea of emotional
sincerity against the unremitting, pervasive, masturbatory manipu-
lations of "scientific" Publicity, and, what is the same thing, commercially supplied popular art?

"In America a fellow can get ahead. Birth don't matter, education
don't matter. It's all getting ahead." In the close of *The Forty-second
Parallel* we see America welcoming an escape from this "getting
ahead," a "meaning" with which to exorcise the void, in the War.
Nineteen-nineteen gives us the War. The second part of the trilogy
is decidedly less lively than the first. For one thing, the monotony of
this world without religion, morality, art or culture is here, perhaps
inevitably, emphasized. And this leads us to the more general
question: What is lacking in the work as a whole (so far as we have
it)?—why, in spite of its complete and rare seriousness, does it fall
so decidedly short of being great?

For answer we have the state of civilization it celebrates. "I guess
all he needs is to go to work and get a sense of values," says a character in *Manhattan Transfer*, exemplifying one of the author's best
ironic effects. The comment on the prescription is the society portrayed: what kind of a sense of values can one acquire, what does
a sense of values mean, in such an environment? The artistic shortcomings of Mr. Dos Passos' most ambitious work (which is not, like
Manhattan Transfer, held together by the topographical limits of
the setting) might thus be, not merely excused as inevitable, but
extolled as propagandist virtues: they are necessary to a work that
exhibits the decay of capitalistic society.

The argument, of course, would be specious. And the point in view might be made most effectively by reframing the question to run: What is lacking in the work as propaganda? This question is answered by asking what it is that Mr. Dos Passos offers us in the way of hope. The suggestion of hope, if it is one, that *Nineteen-nineteen* ends upon is revolution. Whether Mr. Dos Passos intends irony will, perhaps, be made plain in the last volume of the trilogy; but, as it is, the promise must appear as ironical as that upon which *The Forty-second Parallel* closed. Someone in *Nineteen-nineteen* says: "It will take some huge wave of hope like a revolution to make me feel any self-respect ever again." Such a wave of hope, in a world inhabited by Mr. Dos Passos' characters, would, it must seem, be of much the same order as the wave engendered by the outbreak of the war. His revolutionaries are as inadequate, as much "tin mechanical toys, all hollow inside," as his other persons. He plainly realizes this where they are intellectuals; where they are proletarians there is something embarrassingly like sentimentality in his attitude.

It may be that the concluding volume of the trilogy will show this last comment to be unfair in its implications. And perhaps comment on the inadequacy of individuals is discounted by Mr. Dos Passos' philosophy. Nevertheless a literary critic must venture the further judgment that the shortcomings of the work both as art and propaganda are related to a certain insufficiency in it when it is considered as an expression of personality (which on any theory a work of art must in some sense be). It is more than a superficial analogy when the technique is likened to that of the film. The author might be said to conceive his function as selective photography and "montage." That this method does not admit sufficiently of the presence of the artist's personal consciousness the device called "The Camera Eye" seems to recognize—it at any rate seems to do little else. What this judgment amounts to is that the work does not express an adequate realization of the issues it offers to deal with.

How far the defect is due to the method, and how far it lies in the consciousness behind the method, one cannot presume to determine. But Mr. Dos Passos, though he exhibits so overwhelmingly the results of disintegration and decay, shows nothing like an adequate awareness of—or concern for—what has been lost. Perhaps we have here the disability corresponding to the advantage he enjoys as an American. In America the Western process has gone furthest, and what has been lost is virtually forgotten. Certainly Mr. Dos Passos seems to share—it is a confirming sign—the attitude towards art and literature that so curiously qualifies the intelligence and penetration of Mr. Edmund Wilson's *Axel's Castle* (a book which only an American could have written). "Art," for the aspirant to "culture" in *The Forty-second Parallel,* is "something ivory-white and very pure and noble and distant and sad." The mind behind "The Camera Eye" seems to conceive of "culture" after much the same fashion in rejecting it: ". . . grow cold with culture like a cup of tea forgotten between an incenseburner and a volume of Oscar Wilde."

What has disintegrated—this is the point—is not merely "bourgeois" or "capitalist" civilization; it is the organic community. Instead of the rural community and the town-community we have, almost universally, suburbanism (for the nature and significance of suburbanism see the article by Mr. W. L. Cuttle in *The Universities Review* for October, 1931). The organic community has virtually disappeared, and with it the only basis for a genuine national culture; so nearly disappeared that when one speaks of the old popular culture that existed in innumerable local variations people cannot grasp what one means. This is no place to try and explain. But let them re-read *The Pilgrim's Progress* and consider its significance, *Change in the Village, The Wheelwright's Shop,* and the other works of George Bourne, and, say, Cecil Torr's *Small Talk at Wreyland,* and then, for a commentary on the passing of the old order, go to *Middletown.* The education in reading offered, for instance, under the auspices of the W.E.A., is a substitute, and, as everyone who has lent a hand in it must at some time have realized, a substitute that can hardly begin to negotiate with the student's needs, and so must almost inevitably tend to a conception of Art as "something ivory-white and very pure and distant and sad." (It is relevant here to note that Mr. J. H. Fowler, in *The Art of Teach-*

ing English, holds Ruskin to be "the greatest writer of English prose that ever lived.")

The memory of the old order, the old ways of life, must be the chief hint for, the directing incitement towards, a new, if ever there is to be a new. It is the memory of a human normality or naturalness (one may recognise it as such without ignoring what has been gained in hygiene, public humanity and comfort). Whether, in a world of continually developing machine technique, a new order will ever be able to grow may seem doubtful. But without the faith that one might be achieved there can hardly be hope in revolution. "There'd be gaiety for the workers then, after the revolution," says someone in *Manhattan Transfer.* And in *The Forty-second Parallel* we read of "quiet men who wanted a house with a porch to putter around, and a fat wife to cook for them, a few drinks and cigars, and a garden to dig in." This is all that Mr. Dos Passos suggests (as yet) concerning the way in which meaning is to be restored to the agonized vacuity that it is his distinction to convey so potently.

It seems to me that the more one sympathizes with his propagandist intention, the more should one be concerned to stress what is lacking in his presentment of it. To hope that, if the mechanics of civilization (so to speak) are perfected, the other problems (those which Mr. Dos Passos is mainly preoccupied with) will solve themselves, is vain: "you know," says someone in *Nineteen-nineteen,* "the kind of feeling when everything you've wanted crumbles in your fingers as you grasp it." Men and women might, of course, find happiness—or release from unhappiness—as perfect accessory machines. But that is hardly a hope for a propagandist to offer.

John Dos Passos: The Poet and the World

by Malcolm Cowley

John Dos Passos is in reality two novelists. One of them is a late-Romantic, an individualist, an esthete moving about the world in a portable ivory tower; the other is a collectivist, a radical historian of the class struggle. These two authors have collaborated in all his books, but the first had the larger share in *Three Soldiers* and *Manhattan Transfer*. The second, in his more convincing fashion, has written most of *The 42nd Parallel* and almost all of *1919*. The difference between the late-Romantic and the radical Dos Passos is important not only in his own career: it also helps to explain the recent course of American fiction.

The late-Romantic tendency in his novels goes back to his years in college. After graduating from a good preparatory school, Dos Passos entered Harvard in 1912, at the beginning of a period which was later known as that of the Harvard esthetes. I have described this period elsewhere, in reviewing the poems of E. E. Cummings, but I did not discuss the ideas which underlay its picturesque manifestations, its mixture of incense, patchouli and gin, its erudition displayed before barroom mirrors, its dreams in the Cambridge subway of laurel-crowned Thessalian dancers. The esthetes themselves were not philosophers; they did not seek to define their attitude; but most of them would have subscribed to the following propositions:

That the cultivation and expression of his own sensibility are the only justifiable ends for a poet.

That originality is his principal virtue.

"John Dos Passos: The Poet and the World" by Malcolm Cowley. From *The New Republic*, LXX (April 27, 1932), pp. 303–5; and LXXXVIII (September 9, 1936), p. 34.

That society is hostile, stupid and unmanageable: it is the world of the philistines, from which it is the poet's duty and privilege to remain aloof.

That the poet is always misunderstood by the world. He should, in fact, deliberately make himself misunderstandable, for the greater glory of art.

That he triumphs over the world, at moments, by mystically including it within himself: these are his moments of *ecstasy*, to be provoked by any means in his power—alcohol, drugs, madness or saintliness, venery, suicide.

That art, the undying expression of such moments, exists apart from the world; it is the poet's revenge on society.

That the past has more dignity than the present.

There are a dozen other propositions which might be added to this unwritten manifesto, but the ideas I have listed were those most generally held, and they are sufficient to explain the intellectual atmosphere of the young men who read *The Hill of Dreams,* and argued about St. Thomas in Boston bars, and contributed to *The Harvard Monthly.* The attitude was not confined to one college and one magazine. It was often embodied in *The Dial,* which for some years was almost a postgraduate edition of *The Monthly;* it existed in earlier publications like *The Yellow Book* and *La Revue Blanche;* it has a history, in fact, almost as long as that of the upper middle class under capitalism. For the last half-century it has furnished the intellectual background of poems and essays without number. It would seem to preclude, in its adherents, the objectivity that is generally associated with good fiction; yet the esthetes themselves sometimes wrote novels, as did their predecessors all over the world. Such novels, in fact, are still being published, and favorably criticised: "Mr. Zed has written the absorbing story of a talented musician tortured by the petty atmosphere of the society in which he is forced to live. His wife, whom the author portrays with witty malice, prevents him from breaking away. After an unhappy love affair and the failure of his artistic hopes, he commits suicide. . . ."

Such is the plot forever embroidered in the type of fiction that ought to be known as the art novel. There are two essential characters, two antagonists, the Poet and the World. The Poet—who may also be a painter, a violinist, an inventor, an architect or a Centaur —is generally to be identified with the author of the novel, or at least with the novelist's ideal picture of himself. He tries to assert his individuality in despite of the World, which is stupid, unmanageable and usually victorious. Sometimes the Poet triumphs, but the art novelists seem to realize, as a class, that the sort of hero they describe is likely to be defeated in the sort of society which he must face. This society is rarely presented in accurate terms. So little is it endowed with reality, so great is the author's solicitude for the Poet, that we are surprised to see him vanquished by such a shadowy opponent. It is as if we were watching motion pictures in the dark-house of his mind. There are dream pictures, nightmare pictures; at last the walls crash in and the Poet disappears without ever knowing what it was all about; he dies by his own hand, leaving behind him the memory of his ecstatic moments and the bitter story of his failure, now published as a revenge on the world of the philistines.

The art novel has many variations. Often the World is embodied in the Poet's wife, whose social ambitions are the immediate cause of his defeat. Or the wife may be painted in attractive colors: she is married to a mediocre Poet who finally and reluctantly accepts her guidance, abandons his vain struggle for self-expression, and finds that mediocrity has its own consolations, its country clubs and business triumphs—this is the form in which the art novel is offered to readers of *The Saturday Evening Post.* Or again the Poet may be a woman who fights for the same ambitions, under the same difficulties, as her male prototypes. The scene of the struggle may be a town on the Minnesota prairies, an English rectory, an apartment on Washington Square or Beacon Hill; but always the characters are the same; the Poet and the World continue their fatal conflict; the Poet has all our sympathies. And the novelists who use this plot for the thousandth time are precisely those who believe that originality is a writer's chief virtue.

Many are unconscious of this dilemma. The story rises so immediately out of their lives, bursts upon them with such freshness, that they never recognize it as a family tale. Others deliberately face the problem and try to compensate for the staleness of the plot by the originality of their treatment. They experiment with new methods of story-telling—one of which, the stream of consciousness, seems peculiarly fitted to novels of this type. Perhaps they invest their characters with new significance, and rob them of any real significance, by making them symbolic. They adopt new manners, poetic, mystical, learned, witty, allusive or obfuscatory; and often, in token of their original talent, they invent new words and new ways of punctuating simple declarative sentences. Not all their ingenuity is wasted. Sometimes they make valuable discoveries; a few of the art novels, like *The Hill of Dreams*, are among the minor masterpieces of late-Romantic literature; and a very few, like *A Portrait of the Artist as a Young Man*, are masterpieces pure and simple.

Dos Passos' early books are neither masterpieces nor are they pure examples of the art novel. The world was always real to him, painfully real; it was never veiled with mysticism and his characters were rarely symbolic. Yet consider the plot of a novel like *Three Soldiers*. A talented young musician, during the War, finds that his sensibilities are being outraged, his aspirations crushed, by society as embodied in the American army. He deserts after the Armistice and begins to write a great orchestral poem. When the military police come to arrest him, the sheets of music flutter one by one into the spring breeze; and we are made to feel that the destruction of this symphony, this ecstatic song choked off and dispersed on the wind, is the real tragedy of the War. Some years later, in writing *Manhattan Transfer*, Dos Passos seemed to be undertaking a novel of a different type, one which tried to render the color and movement of a whole city; but the book, as it proceeds, becomes the story of Jimmy Herf (the Poet) and Ellen Thatcher (the Poet's wife), and the Poet is once again frustrated by the World: he leaves a Greenwich Village party after a last drink of gin and walks out alone, bareheaded, into the dawn. It is obvious, however, that a new conflict has been superimposed on the old one: the social ideas of the novelist are now at war with his personal emotions, which remain those of *The Dial* and *The Harvard Monthly*. Even in *1919*, this second conflict persists, but less acutely; the emotional values them-

selves are changing, to accord with the ideas; and the book as a
whole belongs to a new category.

1919 is distinguished, first of all, by the very size of the project its
author has undertaken. A long book in itself, containing 473 pages,
it is merely the second chapter, as it were, of a novel which will com-
pare in length with *Ulysses,* perhaps even with *Remembrance of
Things Past.* Like the latter, it is a historical novel dealing with the
yesterday that still exists in the author's memory. It might almost be
called a news novel, since it uses newspaper headlines to suggest the
flow of events, and tells the story of its characters in reportorial fashion. But its chief distinction lies in the author's emphasis. He is not
recounting the tragedy of bewildered John Smith, the rise of ambitious Mary Jones, the efforts of sensitive Richard Robinson to maintain his ideals against the blundering malice of society. Such episodes recur in this novel, but they are seen in perspective. The real
hero of *The 42nd Parallel* and *1919* is society itself, American society
as embodied in forty or fifty representative characters who drift
along with it, struggle to change its course, or merely to find a secure
footing—perhaps they build a raft of wreckage, grow fat on the
refuse floating about them; perhaps they go under in some obscure
eddy—while always the current sweeps them onward toward new
social horizons. In this sense, Dos Passos has written the first American collective novel.

The principal characters are brought forward one at a time; the
story of each is told in bare, straightforward prose. Thus, J. Ward
Moorehouse, born in Wilmington, Delaware, begins his business
career in a real-estate office. He writes songs, marries and divorces
a rich woman, works for a newspaper in Pittsburgh—at the end of
fifty-seven pages he is a successful public-relations counselor em-
barked on a campaign to reconcile labor and capital at the expense
of labor. Joe and Janey Williams are the children of a tugboat captain from Washington, D. C.; Janey studies shorthand; Joe plays
baseball, enlists in the navy, deserts after a brawl and becomes a
merchant seaman. Eleanor Stoddard is a poor Chicago girl who
works at Marshall Field's; she learns how to speak French to her cus-
tomers and order waiters about "with a crisp little refined moneyed

voice." All these characters, first introduced in *The 42nd Parallel*, reappear in *1919*, where they are joined by others: Richard Ellsworth Savage, a Kent School boy who goes to Harvard and writes poetry; Daughter, a warm-hearted flapper from Dallas, Texas; Ben Compton, a spectacled Jew from Brooklyn who becomes a Wobbly. Gradually their careers draw closer together, till finally all of them are caught up in the War.

"This whole goddam war's a gold brick," says Joe Williams. "It ain't on the level, it's crooked from A to Z. No matter how it comes out, fellows like us get the s——y end of the stick, see? Well, what I say is all bets is off . . . every man go to hell in his own way . . . and three strikes is out, see?" Three strikes is out for Joe, when his skull is cracked in a saloon brawl at St. Nazaire, on Armistice night. Daughter is killed in an airplane accident; she provoked it herself in a fit of hysteria after being jilted by Dick Savage—who for his part survives as the shell of a man, all the best of him having died when he decided to join the army and make a career for himself and let his pacifist sentiments go hang. Benny Compton gets ten years in Atlanta prison as a conscientious objector. Everybody in the novel suffers from the War and finds his own way of going to hell—everybody except the people without bowels, the empty people like Eleanor Stoddard and J. Ward Moorehouse, who stuff themselves with the proper sentiments and make the right contacts.

The great events that preceded and followed the Armistice are reflected in the lives of all these people; but Dos Passos has other methods, too, for rendering the sweep of history. In particular he has three technical devices which he uses both to broaden the scope of the novel and to give it a formal unity. The first of these consists of what he calls "Newsreels," a combination of newspaper headlines, stock-market reports, official communiqués and words from popular songs. The Newsreels effectively perform their function in the book, that of giving dates and atmospheres, but in themselves, judged as writing, they are not successful. The second device is a series of nine biographies interspersed through the text. Here are the lives, briefly told, of three middle-class rebels, Jack Reed, Randolph Bourne and Paxton Hibben; of three men of power, Roosevelt, Wilson and

J. P. Morgan; and of three proletarian heroes. All these are successful both in themselves and in relation to the novel as a whole; and
the passage dealing with the Wobbly martyr, Wesley Everest, is as
powerful as anything Dos Passos has ever written.

The "Camera Eye," which is the third device, introduces more
complicated standards of judgment. It consists in the memories of
another character, presumably the author, who has adventures similar to those of his characters, but describes them in a different style,
one which suggests Dos Passos' earlier books. The "Camera Eye"
gives us photographs rich in emotional detail:

> Ponte Decimo   in Ponte Decimo ambulances were parked in a
> moonlit square of bleak stone working-people's houses   hoarfrost
> covered everything   in the little bar the Successful Story Writer
> taught us to drink cognac and maraschino half and half
>   havanuzzerone
>   it turned out he was not writing what he felt he wanted to be writ-
> ing   What can you tell them at home about the war?   it turned
> out he was not wanting what he wrote he wanted to be feel-
> ing   cognac and maraschino   was no longer young   (It made
> us damn sore we greedy for what we felt we wanted tell 'em all they
> lied see new towns go to Genoa)   havanuzzerone?   it turned out
> that he wished he was a naked brown shepherd boy sitting on a hill-
> side playing a flute in the sunlight.

Exactly the same episode, so it happens, is described in Dos Passos'
other manner, his prose manner, during the course of a chapter dealing with Dick Savage:

> That night they parked the convoy in the main square of a godfor-
> saken little burg on the outskirts of Genoa. They went with Shel-
> drake to have a drink in a bar and found themselves drinking with
> the Saturday Evening Post correspondent, who soon began to get
> tight and to say how he envied them their good looks and their san-
> guine youth and idealism. Steve picked him up about everything and
> argued bitterly that youth was the lousiest time in your life, and that
> he ought to be goddam glad he was forty years old and able to write
> about the war instead of fighting in it.

The relative merit of these two passages, as writing, is not an important question. The first is a good enough piece of impressionism, with undertones of E. E. Cummings and Gertrude Stein. The style of the second passage, except for a certain conversational quality, is almost colorless; it happens to be the most effective way of recording a particular series of words and actions; it aspires to no other virtue. The first passage might add something to a book in which, the plot being hackneyed or inconsequential, the emphasis had to be placed on the writing, but *1919* is not a novel of that sort. Again, the Camera Eye may justify itself in the next volume of this trilogy—or tetralogy—by assuming a closer relation to the story and binding together the different groups of characters; but in that case, I hope the style of it will change. So far it has been an element of disunity, a survival of the art novel in the midst of a different type of writing, and one in which Dos Passos excels.

He is, indeed, one of the few writers in whose case an equation can accurately and easily be drawn between social beliefs and artistic accomplishments. When he writes individualistically, with backward glances toward Imagism, Vorticism and the Insurrection of the Word, his prose is sentimental and without real distinction. When he writes as a social rebel, he writes not flawlessly by any means, but with conviction, power and a sense of depth, of striking through surfaces to the real forces beneath them. This last book, in which his political ideas have given shape to his emotions, and only the Camera Eye remains as a vestige of his earlier attitude, is not only the best of all his novels; it is, I believe, a landmark in American fiction.

II

Four years ago in reviewing *1919,* the second volume of John Dos Passos' trilogy, I tried to define two types of fiction that have been especially prominent since the War. An *art novel,* I said, was one that dealt with the opposition between a creatively gifted individual and the community surrounding him—in brief, between the Poet and the World. Usually in books of this type the Poet gets all the attention; he is described admiringly, tenderly, and yet we learn that he is nagged and broken and often, in the end, driven to suicide by an implacably stupid World. Dos Passos' earlier novels had applied this formula, but *The 42nd Parallel* and *1919* belonged to a second category: they were *collective novels,* whose real hero was American society at large, and this fact helped to explain their greater breadth and vigor. I added, however, that certain elements in these later books—and notably the autobiographical passages called the "Camera Eye"—suggested the art novel and therefore seemed out of place.

But after reviewing *The Big Money* and rereading the trilogy as a whole, it seems to me that this judgment has to be partly revised. I no longer believe that the art novel is a "bad" type of fiction (though the philosophy behind it is a bad philosophy for our times), nor do I believe that the collective novel is necessarily a "good" type (though it has advantages for writers trying to present our period of crisis). With more and more collective novels published every year, it is beginning to be obvious that the form in itself does not solve the writer's problems. Indeed, it raises new problems and creates new disadvantages. The collective novelist is tempted to overemphasize the blindness and impotence of individuals caught in the rip tides of history. He is obliged to devote less space to each of his characters, to relate their adventures more hastily, with the result that he always seems to be approaching them from the outside. I can see now that the Camera Eye is a device adopted by Dos Passos in order to supply the "inwardness" that is lacking in his general narrative.

I can see too that although the device is borrowed from the art novel—and indeed is a series of interior monologues resembling parts of Joyce's *Ulysses*—it is not in the least alien to the general plan of the trilogy. For the truth is that the art novel and the collective novel as conceived by Dos Passos are not in fundamental opposition: they are like the two sides of a coin. In the art novel, the emphasis is on the individual, in the collective novel it is on society as a whole; but in both we get the impression that society is stupid

and all-powerful and fundamentally evil. Individuals ought to op-
pose it, but if they do so they are doomed. If, on the other hand, they
reconcile themselves with society and try to get ahead in it, then
they are damned forever, damned to be empty, shrill, destructive in-
sects like Dick Savage and Eleanor Stoddard and J. Ward Moorehouse.

In an earlier novel, *Manhattan Transfer,* there is a paragraph that
states one of Dos Passos' basic perceptions. Ellen Herf, having di-
vorced the hero, decides to marry a rich politician whom she does
not love:

> Through dinner she felt a gradual icy coldness stealing through
> her like novocaine. She had made up her mind. It seemed as if she
> had set the photograph of herself in her own place, forever frozen
> into a single gesture. . . . Everything about her seemed to be grow-
> ing hard and enameled, the air bluestreaked with cigarette smoke
> was turning to glass.

She had made up her mind. . . . Sometimes in reading Dos
Passos it seems that not the nature of the decision but the mere fact
of having reached it is the unforgivable offense. Dick Savage the
ambulance driver decided not to be a pacifist, not to escape into
neutral Spain, and from that moment he is forever frozen into a
single gesture of selfishness and dissipation. Don Stevens the radical
newspaper correspondent decides to be a good Communist, to obey
party orders, and immediately he is stricken with the same paralysis
of the heart. We have come a long way from the strong-willed heroes
of the early nineteenth century—the English heroes, sons of Dick
Whittington, who admired the world of their day and climbed to
the top of it implacably; the French heroes like Julien Sorel and
Rastignac and Monte Cristo who despised their world and yet
learned how to press its buttons and pull its levers. To Dos Passos
the world seems so vicious that any compromise with its standards
turns a hero into a villain. The only characters he seems to like in-
stinctively are those who know they are beaten, but still grit their
teeth and try to hold on. That is the story of Jimmy Herf in *Manhattan Transfer*; to some extent it is also the story of Mary French

and her father and Joe Askew, almost the only admirable characters in *The Big Money*. And the same lesson of dogged, courageous impotence is pointed by the Camera Eye, especially in the admirable passage where the author remembers the execution of Sacco and Vanzetti:

> America our nation has been beaten by strangers who have turned our language inside out who have taken the clean words our fathers spoke and made them slimy and foul
>   their hired men sit on the judge's bench they sit back with their feet on the tables under the dome of the State House they are ignorant of our beliefs they have the dollars the guns the armed forces the power-plant . . .
>   all right we are two nations

"The hired men with guns stand ready to shoot," he says in another passage, this one dealing with his visit to the striking miners in Kentucky. "We have only words against POWER SUPERPOWER." And these words that serve as our only weapons against the machine guns and tear gas of the invaders, these words of the vanquished nation are only that America in developing from pioneer democracy into monopoly capitalism has followed a road that leads toward sterility and slavery. Our world is evil, and yet we are powerless to change or direct it. The sensitive individual should cling to his own standards, and yet he is certain to go under. Thus, the final message of Dos Passos' three collective novels is similar to that of his earlier novels dealing with maladjusted artists. Thus, for all the vigor of *1919* and *The Big Money*, they leave us wondering whether the author hasn't overstated his case. For all their scope and richness, they fail to express one side of contemporary life—the will to struggle ahead, the comradeship in struggle, the consciousness of new men and new forces continually rising. Although we may be for the moment a beaten nation, the fight is not over.

Dos Passos and the U. S. A.

by T. K. Whipple

The choice of the ambitious title "U. S. A." for the volume which brings together Dos Passos's "The 42nd Parallel," "Nineteen-Nineteen," and "The Big Money" looks as if it might be intended to stake out a claim on the fabulous "great American novel." And Dos Passos's claim is not a weak one. A single book could hardly be more inclusive than his: in the stories of his main characters he covers most parts of the country during the first three decades of the twentieth century. His people have considerable social diversity, ranging from Mac, the I. W. W. typesetter, and Joe Williams, the feckless sailor, to Ben Compton, the radical leader, Eleanor Stoddard, the successful decorator, Margo Dowling, the movie star, and J. Ward Moorehouse, the big publicity man. The background of the panorama is filled out with "newsreels" of newspaper headlines, popular songs, and the like, with the autobiographic "camera eye" which gives snatches of Dos Passos's own experience, and with a series of biographical portraits of representative men—Debs, Edison, Wilson, Joe Hill, Ford, Veblen, Hearst, and twenty more. Probably no other American novel affords a picture so varied and so comprehensive.

Furthermore, the picture is rendered with extraordinary vividness and brilliance of detail, especially of sensory detail. Sights and sounds and above all smells abound until the reader is forced to wonder that so many people, of such different sorts, are all so constantly aware of what their eyes and ears and noses report to them: might not some of them, one asks, more often get absorbed in medi-

"Dos Passos and the U. S. A." by T. K. Whipple. From *The Nation*, February 19, 1938, pp. 210–12. Copyright © 1938 by *The Nation*. Reprinted by permission of *The Nation*.

tation or memory or planning or reverie? But it is no part of Dos
Passos's scheme to spend much time inside his characters' heads; he
tells, for the most part, what an outsider would have seen or heard—
gestures, actions, talk, as well as the surroundings. The result is a
tribute to the keenness of the author's observation—not only of
colors, noises, and odors but, even more important, of human behavior and of American speech. People as well as things are sharp
and distinct.

Nor does the presentation lack point and significance. As the
book goes on, the U. S. A. develops, with the precision of a vast and
masterly photograph, into a picture of a business world in its final
ripeness, ready to fall into decay. Though Dos Passos does not call
himself a Marxist—and would seem in fact not to be one—his point
of view is unmistakably radical. The class struggle is present as a
minor theme; the major theme is the vitiation and degradation of
character in such a civilization. Those who prostitute themselves
and succeed are most completely corrupted; the less hard and less
self-centered are baffled and beaten; those who might have made
good workers are wasted; the radicals experience internal as well as
external defeat. No one attains any real satisfaction. Disintegration
and frustration are everywhere. The whole presentation leads to the
summary: "Life is a shambles." Perhaps there are implications that
it need not be; but no doubt is left that actually it is.

These generalities, when stated as generalities, have of course become the trite commonplaces of a whole school of literature. But
actual people shown going through the process of victimization can
never become trite or commonplace; the spectacle must always be
pitiful and terrible. And no one, I should suppose, could look on
Dos Passos's picture wholly untouched and unmoved. But still one
might ask whether he has quite achieved the tragic effect which presumably he aimed at.

To complain that the picture is one-sided may appear captious
and unreasonable, and in one sense of "one-sided" it is. The whole
truth about a hundred million people throughout thirty years cannot be told in fifteen hundred—or in fifteen million—pages. The
novelist has to select what he considers representative and character-

istic persons and events, and if Dos Passos has chosen to omit big business men, farmers, and factory workers, and to dwell chiefly on midway people in somewhat ambiguous positions—intellectuals, decorators, advertising men—perhaps that is his privilege. The question is whether this picture of his, which is surely extensive enough as novels go, is entirely satisfactory within the limitations which must be granted. How close does "U. S. A." come to being a great American novel? That it comes within hailing distance is proved by the fact that it has already been so hailed; indeed, it comes close enough so that the burden of proof is on those who would deny the title. Yet to grant it offhand would be premature.

On one point at least everyone probably agrees: that the biographical portraits are magnificent, and are the best part of the book. But wherein are they superior? Is it not that these portraits have a greater depth and solidity than Dos Passos's fictional characterizations—a more complete humanity? If so, the implication must be that his creation of character is not complete. And indeed when Mac is put beside Big Bill Haywood, or Ben Compton beside Joe Hill and Jack Reed, or Margo Dowling beside Isadora Duncan, the contrast is unflattering to Dos Passos's powers as a novelist. There is more human reality in the 10 pages given to Henry Ford than in the 220 given to Charley Anderson. Nor is the explanation that the real people are exceptional, the fictitious ones ordinary, satisfactory: some of the fictitious ones are supposed to be leaders; and besides it is a novelist's business so to choose and treat his imagined characters as to reveal his themes in their utmost extension, not at their flattest. No; the contrast has nothing to do with the positions people occupy; it is a fundamental matter of the conception of human nature and the portrayal of it in literature.

In thinking of this contrast, one notices first that the real men have a far better time of it in the world, that they do find a good many genuine satisfactions, that even when they fail—when they are jailed like Debs or shot down like Joe Hill—they are not wholly defeated. Inside them is some motive power which keeps them going to the end. Some of them swim with the stream and some against it, but they all swim; they all put up a fight. They all have persistent ruling passions. Furthermore, they are all complex and many-sided, full of contradictions and tensions and conflicts. They have minds, consciousness, individuality, and personality.

Not that all these things are entirely lacking in the fictitious characters—Dos Passos is too good a novelist for that—but they do appear only in a much lower degree, played down, degraded, reduced to a minimum. As a result, the consciousness of these people is of a relatively low order. True, they are aware with an abnormal keenness of their sensations, but is not this sensory awareness the most elementary form of consciousness? On the other hand, these folk can hardly be said to think at all, and their feelings are rather sharp transitory reactions than long-continuing dominant emotions. Above all, they are devoid of will or purpose, helplessly impelled hither and yon by the circumstances of the moment. They have no strength of resistance. They are weak at the very core of personality, the power to choose. Now it may be that freedom of choice is an illusion, but if so it is an inescapable one, and even the most deterministic and behavioristic novelist cannot omit it or minimize it without denaturing human beings. When the mainspring of choice is weakened or left out, the conflicts and contradictions of character lose their virtue and significance, and personality almost disappears. Dos Passos often gives this effect: that in his people there is, so to speak, nobody much at home, or that he is holding out on us and that more must be happening than he is willing to let on. This deficiency shows itself most plainly in the personal relations of his characters—they are hardly persons enough to sustain real relations with one another, any more than billiard balls do—and in his treatment of crises, which he is apt to dispose of in some such way as: "They had a row so that night he took the train. . . ."

The final effect is one of banality—that human beings and human life are banal. Perhaps this is the effect Dos Passos aimed at, but that it is needless and even false is proved by the biographical portraits, in which neither the men nor their lives are ever banal. The same objection holds, therefore, to Dos Passos's whole social picture as to his treatment of individuals, that he has minimized something vital and something which ought to be made much of—namely, forces in conflict. Society is hardly just rotting away and drifting apart; the destructive forces are tremendously powerful and well organized, and so are the creative ones. Furthermore, they are inextricably intermingled in institutions and in individuals. If Dos Passos is forced, by sheer fact, to present them so when he writes of Ford and Steinmetz and Morgan, why should he make little of them in his fiction? Is it to illustrate a preconceived and misleading notion that life nowadays is a silly and futile "shambles"?

One might hope, but in vain, to find the answer in the autobiographic "camera eye." To be sure, the author there appears as the extremest type of Dos Passos character, amazingly sensitive to impressions, and so amazingly devoid of anything else that most of the "camera eye" is uninteresting in the extreme. The effect of this self-portrait is further heightened by the brief prologue which introduces "U. S. A.": an account of a young man, plainly the author himself, who "walks by himself searching through the crowd with greedy eyes, greedy ears taut to hear, by himself, alone," longing to share everybody's life, finding his only link with other people in listening to their talk. If the obvious conclusion could be accepted that Dos Passos had been never a participant but always a mere onlooker hungry for participation, so that he had to depend only on observation from outside, it would explain much. But such is not the fact; he took part in the World War and in the Sacco-Vanzetti case and other activities. He has been no mere spectator of the world. Moreover, he must have had powerful and lasting purposes and emotions to have written his books, and it is hardly credible that he has done so little thinking as he makes out. His self-portrait must be heinously incomplete, if only because he is a real man. But it is possible that he may have chosen to suppress some things in himself and in his writing, and that he may have acquired a distrust of thought and feeling and will which has forced him back upon sensations as the only reliable part of experience. Some such process seems to have taken place in many writers contemporary with him, resulting in a kind of spiritual drought, and in a fear lest they betray themselves or be betrayed by life. Perhaps the disillusionment of the war had something to do with it, but more probably a partial view and experience of our present society are responsible.

According to any view, that society, in all conscience, is grim enough, but not banal, not undramatic. Dos Passos has reduced what ought to be a tale of full-bodied conflicts to an epic of disintegration and frustration. That reduction—*any* reduction—is open to objection, because it is an imperfect account of human beings and human society that does not present forces working in opposition. In that sense "U. S. A." is one-sided, whereas life and good literature are two-sided or many-sided. In a word, what we want is a dialectic treatment of people and the world. Dos Passos does not call himself a Marxist; if he were more of one, he might have written a better novel. The biographical portraits are the best part of his book because they are the most nearly Marxist, showing the dynamic contradictions of our time in the only way they can be shown—namely, as they occur in the minds and lives of whole men. Nothing will do, in the end, but the whole man.

The America of John Dos Passos

by Lionel Trilling

U. S. A. is far more impressive than even its three impressive parts—*42nd Parallel, 1919, The Big Money*—might have led one to expect. It stands as the important American novel of the decade, on the whole more satisfying than anything else we have. It lacks any touch of eccentricity; it is startlingly normal; at the risk of seeming paradoxical one might say that it is exciting because of its quality of cliché: here are comprised the judgments about modern American life that many of us have been living on for years.

Yet too much must not be claimed for this book. To-day we are inclined to make literature too important, to estimate the writer's function at an impossibly high rate, to believe that he can encompass and resolve all the contradictions, and to demand that he should. We forget that, by reason of his human nature, he is likely to win the intense perception of a single truth at the cost of a relative blindness to other truths. We expect a single man to give us all the answers and produce the "synthesis." And then when the writer, hailed for giving us much, is discovered to have given us less than everything, we turn from him in a reaction of disappointment: he has given us nothing. A great deal has been claimed for Dos Passos and it is important, now that *U. S. A.* is completed, to mark off the boundaries of its enterprise and see what it does not do so that we may know what it does do.

One thing *U. S. A.* does not do is originate; it confirms but does not advance and it summarizes but does not suggest. There is no accent or tone of feeling that one is tempted to make one's own and carry further in one's own way. No writer, I think, will go to school to Dos Passos, and readers, however much they may admire him will not stand in the relation to him in which they stand, say, to Stendhal or Henry James or even E. M. Forster. Dos Passos' plan is greater than its result in feeling; his book *tells* more than it *is*. Yet what it tells, and tells with accuracy, subtlety and skill, is enormously important and no one else has yet told it half so well.

Nor is *U. S. A.* as all-embracing as its admirers claim. True, Dos Passos not only represents a great national scene but he embodies, as I have said, the cultural tradition of the intellectual Left. But he does not encompass—does not pretend to encompass in this book— all of either. Despite his title, he is consciously selective of his America and he is, as I shall try to show, consciously corrective of the cultural tradition from which he stems.

Briefly and crudely, this cultural tradition may be said to consist of the following beliefs, which are not so much formulations of theory or principles of action as they are emotional tendencies: that the collective aspects of life may be distinguished from the individual aspects; that the collective aspects are basically important and are good; that the individual aspects are, or should be, of small interest and that they contain a destructive principle; that the fate of the individual is determined by social forces; that the social forces now dominant are evil; that there is a conflict between the dominant social forces and other, better, rising forces; that it is certain or very likely that the rising forces will overcome the now dominant ones. *U. S. A.* conforms to some but not to all of these assumptions. The lack of any protagonists in the trilogy, the equal attention given to many people, have generally been taken to represent Dos Passos' recognition of the importance of the collective idea. The book's historical apparatus indicates the author's belief in social determination. And there can be no slightest doubt of Dos Passos' attitude to the dominant forces of our time: he hates them.

But Dos Passos modifies the tradition in three important respects. Despite the collective elements of his trilogy, he puts a peculiar importance upon the individual. Again, he avoids propounding any sharp conflict between the dominant forces of evil and the rising forces of good; more specifically, he does not write of a class struggle, nor is he much concerned with the notion of class in the political sense. Finally, he is not at all assured of the eventual triumph of good; he pins no faith on any force or party—indeed he is almost alone of the novelists of the Left (Silone is the only other one that comes to mind) in saying that the creeds and idealisms of the Left may bring corruption quite as well as the greeds and cynicisms of the established order; he has refused to cry "Allons! the road lies before us," and, in short, his novel issues in despair.—And it is this despair of Dos Passos' book which has made his two ablest critics, Malcolm Cowley and T. K. Whipple, seriously temper their admiration. Mr. Cowley says: "They [the novels comprising *U. S. A.*] give us an extraordinarily diversified picture of contemporary life, but they fail to include at least one side of it—the will to struggle ahead, the comradeship in struggle, the consciousness of new men and new forces continually rising." And Mr. Whipple: "Dos Passos has reduced what ought to be a tale of full-bodied conflicts to an epic of disintegration." [1]

These critics are saying that Dos Passos has not truly observed the political situation. Whether he has or not, whether his despair is objectively justifiable, cannot, with the best political will in the world, be settled on paper. We hope he has seen incorrectly; he himself must hope so. But there is also an implicit meaning in the objections which, if the writers themselves did not intend it, many readers will derive, and if not from Mr. Whipple and Mr. Cowley then from the book itself: that the emotion in which *U. S. A.* issues is negative to the point of being politically harmful.

But to discover a political negativism in the despair of *U. S. A.* is to subscribe to a naive conception of human emotion and of the literary experience. It is to assert that the despair of a literary work must inevitably engender despair in the reader. Actually, of course, it need do nothing of the sort. To rework the old Aristotelian insight, it may bring about a catharsis of an already existing despair. But

1. [For the articles in question by Whipple and Cowley see pp. 87 and 76 of this volume.—Ed.]

more important: the word "despair" all by itself (or any other such general word or phrase) can never characterize the emotion the artist is dealing with. There are many kinds of despair and what is really important is what goes along with the general emotion denoted by the word. Despair with its wits about it is very different from despair that is stupid; despair that is an abandonment of illusion is very different from despair which generates tender new cynicisms. The "heartbreak" of *Heartbreak House,* for example, is the beginning of new courage and I can think of no more useful *political* job for the literary man today than, by the representation of despair, to cauterize the exposed soft tissue of too-easy hope.

Even more than the despair, what has disturbed the radical admirers of Dos Passos' work is his appearance of indifference to the idea of the class struggle. Mr. Whipple correctly points out that the characters of *U. S. A.* are all "midway people in somewhat ambiguous positions." Thus, there are no bankers or industrialists (except incidentally) but only J. Ward Morehouse, their servant; there are no factory workers (except, again, incidentally), no farmers, but only itinerant workers, individualistic mechanics, actresses, interior decorators.

This, surely, is a limitation in a book that has had claimed for it a complete national picture. But when we say limitation we may mean just that or we may mean falsification, and I do not think that Dos Passos has falsified. The idea of class is not simple but complex. Socially it is extremely difficult to determine. It cannot be determined, for instance, by asking individuals to what class they belong; nor is it easy to convince them that they belong to one class or another. We may, to be sure, demonstrate the idea of class at income-extremes or function-extremes, but when we leave these we must fall back upon the criterion of "interest"—by which we must mean *real* interest ("real will" in the Rousseauian sense) and not what people say or think they want. Even the criterion of action will not determine completely the class to which people belong. Class, then, is a useful but often undetermined category of political and social thought. The political leader and the political theorist will make use of it in ways different from those of the novelist. For the former the important thing is people's perception that they are of one class or another and their resultant action. For the latter the interesting and suggestive things are likely to be the moral paradoxes that result from the conflict between real and apparent interest. And the "midway people" of Dos Passos represent this moral-paradoxical aspect of class. They are a great fact in American life. It is they who show the symptoms of cultural change. Their movement from social group to social group—from class to class, if you will—makes for the uncertainty of their moral codes, their confusion, their indecision. Almost more than the people of fixed class, they are at the mercy of the social stream because their interests cannot be clear to them and give them direction. If Dos Passos has omitted the class struggle, as Mr. Whipple and Mr. Cowley complain, it is only the external class struggle he has left out; within his characters the class struggle is going on constantly.

This, perhaps, is another way of saying that Dos Passos is primarily concerned with morality, with personal morality. The national, collective, social elements of his trilogy should be seen not as a bid for completeness but rather as a great setting, brilliantly delineated, for his moral interest. In his novels, as in actual life, "conditions" supply the opportunity for personal moral action. But if Dos Passos is a social historian, as he is so frequently said to be, he is that in order to be a more complete moralist. It is of the greatest significance that for him the barometer of social breakdown is not suffering through economic deprivation but always moral degeneration through moral choice.

This must be said in the face of Mr. Whipple's description of Dos Passos' people as "devoid of will or purpose, helplessly impelled hither and yon by the circumstances of the moment. They have no strength of resistance. They are weak at the very core of personality, the power to choose." These, it would seem, are scarcely the characters with which the moralist can best work. But here we must judge not only by the moral equipment of the characters (and it is not at all certain that Mr. Whipple's description is correct: choice of action

is seldom made as the result of Socratic dialectic) but by the novelist's idea of morality—the nature of his judgments and his estimate
of the power of circumstance.

Dos Passos' morality is concerned not so much with the utility
of an action as with the quality of the person who performs it. *What*
his people do is not so important as *how* they do it, or what they
become by doing it. We despise J. Ward Morehouse not so much for
his creation of the labor-relations board, his support of the war,
his advertising of patent-medicines, though these are despicable
enough; we despise him rather for the words he uses as he does these
things, for his self-deception, the tone and style he generates. We
despise G. H. Barrow, the labor-faker, not because he betrays labor;
we despise him because he is mealy-mouthed and talks about "the
art of living" when he means concupiscence. But we do not despise
the palpable fraud, Doc Bingham, because, though he lies to everyone else, he does not lie to himself.

The moral assumption on which Dos Passos seems to work was
expressed by John Dewey some thirty years ago; there are certain
moral situations, Dewey says, where we cannot decide between the
ends; we are forced to make our moral choice in terms of our preference for one kind of character or another: "What sort of an agent,
of a person shall he be? This is the question finally at stake in any
genuinely moral situation: What shall the agent *be?* What sort of
character shall he assume? On its face, the question is what he shall
do, shall he act for this or that end. But the incompatibility of the
ends forces the issue back into the questions of the kind of selfhood,
of agency, involved in the respective ends." One can imagine that
this method of moral decision does not have meaning for all times
and cultures. Although dilemmas exist in every age, we do not find
Antigone settling her struggle between family and state by a reference to the kind of character she wants to be, nor Orestes settling his
in that way; and so with the medieval dilemma of wife vs. friend, or
the family oath of vengeance vs. the feudal oath of allegiance. But
for our age with its intense self-consciousness and its uncertain
moral codes, the reference to the quality of personality does have
meaning, and the greater the social flux the more frequent will be

the interest in qualities of character rather than in the rightness of the end.

The modern novel, with its devices for investigating the quality of character, is the aesthetic form almost specifically called forth to exercise this modern way of judgment. The novelist goes where the law cannot go; he tells the truth where the formulations of even the subtlest ethical theorist cannot. He turns the moral values inside out to question the worth of the deed by looking not at its actual outcome but at its tone and style. He is subversive of dominant morality and under his influence we learn to praise what dominant morality condemns; he reminds us that benevolence may be aggression, that the highest idealism may corrupt. Finally, he gives us the models of the examples by which, half-unconsciously, we make our own moral selves.

Dos Passos does not primarily concern himself with the burly sinners who inherit the earth. His people are those who sin against themselves and for him the wages of sin is death—of the spirit. The whole Dos Passos morality and the typical Dos Passos fate are expressed in Burns' quatrain:

> I waive the quantum o' the sin,
>   The hazard of concealing;
> But, och! it hardens a' within
>   And petrifies the feeling!

In the trilogy physical death sometimes follows upon this petrifaction of the feeling but only as its completion. Only two people die without petrifying, Joe Williams and Daughter, who kept in their inarticulate way a spark of innocence, generosity and protest. Idealism does not prevent the consequences of sinning against oneself and Mary French with her devotion to the working class and the Communist Party, with her courage and "sacrifice" is quite as dead as Richard Savage who inherits Morehouse's mantle, and she is almost as much to blame.

It is this element of blame, of responsibility, that exempts Dos Passos from Malcolm Cowley's charge of being in some part committed to the morality of what Cowley calls the Art Novel—the story of the Poet and the World, the Poet always sensitive and right, the World always crass and wrong. An important element of Dos Passos' moral conception is that, although the World does sin against his characters, the characters themselves are very often as wrong as the World. There is no need to enter the theological pur- lieus to estimate how much responsibility Dos Passos puts upon them and whether this is the right amount. Clearly, however, he holds people like Savage, Fainy McCreary and Eveline Hutchins accountable in some important part for their own fates and their own ignobility.

The morality of Dos Passos, then, is a romantic morality. Per- haps this is calling it a bad name; people say they have got tired of a morality concerned with individuals "saving" themselves and "realizing" themselves. Conceivably only Dos Passos' aggressive con- temporaneity has kept them from seeing how very similar is his morality to, say, Browning's—the moment to be snatched, the cru- cial choice to be made, and if it is made on the wrong (the safe) side, the loss of human quality, so that instead of a man we have a Suc- cess and instead of two lovers a Statue and a Bust in the public square. But too insistent a cry against the importance of the indi- vidual quality is a sick cry—as sick as the cry of "Something to live for" as a motivation of political choice. Among members of a party the considerations of solidarity, discipline and expedience are claimed to replace all others and moral judgment is left to history; among liberals, the idea of social determination, on no good ground, appears tacitly to exclude the moral concern: witness the nearly complete conspiracy of silence or misinterpretation that greeted Silone's *Bread and Wine,* which said not a great deal more than that personal and moral—and eventually political—problems were not settled by membership in a revolutionary party. It is not at all cer- tain that it is political wisdom to ignore what so much concerns the novelist. In the long run is not the political choice fundamentally a choice of personal quality?

Dos Passos, Society, and the Individual

by Alfred Kazin

A chapter in the moral history of modern American writing does come to an end with Hemingway and the lost generation, and nowhere can this be more clearly seen than in the work of John Dos Passos, who rounds out the story of that generation and carries its values into the social novel of the thirties. For what is so significant about Dos Passos is that though he is a direct link between the post-war decade and the crisis novel of the depression period, the defeatism of the lost generation has been slowly and subtly transferred by him from persons to society itself. It is society that becomes the hero of his work, society that suffers the anguish and impending sense of damnation that the lost-generation individualists had suffered alone before. For him the lost generation becomes all the lost generations from the beginning of modern time in America—all who have known themselves to be lost in the fires of war or struggling up the icy slopes of modern capitalism. The tragic "I" has become the tragic inclusive "we" of modern society; the pace of sport, of the separate peace and the separate death, has become the pounding rhythm of the industrial machine. The central beliefs of his generation, though they have a different source in Dos Passos and a different expression, remain hauntingly the same. Working in politics and technology as Fitzgerald worked in the high world and Hemingway in war and sport, Dos Passos comes out with all his equations zero. They are almost too perfectly zero, and always uneasy and reluctantly defeatist. But the record of his novels from

"Dos Passos, Society, and the Individual" (editor's title). From "All the Lost Generations" in *On Native Grounds,* pp. 341–59, copyright 1942, 1970, by Alfred Kazin. Reprinted by permission of Harcourt Brace Jovanovich, Inc.

One Man's Initiation to *Adventures of a Young Man,* whatever the new faith revealed in his hymn to the American democratic tradition in *The Ground We Stand On,* is the last essential testimony of his generation, and in many respects the most embittered.

Dos Passos's zero is not the "nada hail nada full of nada" of Hemingway's most famous period, the poetically felt nihilism and immersion in nothingness; nor is it the moody and ambiguous searching of Fitzgerald. The conviction of tragedy that rises out of his work is the steady protest of a sensitive democratic conscience against the tyranny and the ugliness of society, against the failure of a complete human development under industrial capitalism; it is the protest of a man who can participate formally in the struggles of society as Hemingway and Fitzgerald never do. To understand Dos Passos's social interests is to appreciate how much he differs from the others of his generation, and yet how far removed he is from the Socialist crusader certain Marxist critics once saw in him. For what is central in Dos Passos is not merely the fascination with the total operations of society, but his unyielding opposition to all its degradations. He cannot separate the "I" and society absolutely from each other, like Hemingway, for though he is essentially even less fraternal in spirit, he is too much the conscious political citizen. But the "I" remains as spectator and victim, and it is that conscientious intellectual self that one hears in all his work, up to the shy and elusive autobiography in the "Camera Eye" sections of *U.S.A.* That human self in Dos Passos is the Emersonian individual, not Hemingway's agonist; he is the arbiter of existence, always a little chill, a little withdrawn (everything in Dos Passos radiates around the scrutiny of the camera eye), not the sentient, suffering center of it. He is man believing and trusting in the Emersonian "self-trust" when all else fails him, man taking his stand on individual integrity against the pressures of society. But he is not Hemingway's poetic man. What Emerson once said of himself in his journal is particularly true of Dos Passos: he likes Man, not men.

Dos Passos certainly came closer to Socialism than most artists in his generation; yet it is significant that no novelist in America has written more somberly of the dangers to individual integrity in a centrally controlled society. Spain before the war had meant for Hemingway the bullfighters, Pamplona, the golden wine; for Dos Passos it had meant the Spanish Anarchists and the Quixotic dream he described so affectionately in his early travel book, *Rosinante to the Road Again*. Yet where Hemingway found his "new hope" in the Spanish Civil War, Dos Passos saw in that war not merely the struggle into which his mind had entered as a matter of course, the agony of the Spain with which he had always felt spiritual ties, but the symbolic martyrdom of Glenn Spotswood, the disillusioned former Communist, at the hands of the OGPU in Spain in *Adventures of a Young Man*. Hemingway could at least write *For Whom the Bell Tolls* as the story of Robert Jordan's education; Dos Passos had to write his Spanish novel as the story of Glenn Spotswood's martyrdom. And what is so significant in Dos Passos's work always is individual judgment and martyrdom, the judgment that no fear can prevent his heroes from making on society, the martyrdom that always waits for them at its hands. That last despairing cry of Glenn Spotswood's in the prison of the Loyalists—"I, Glenn Spotswood, being of sound mind and emprisoned body, do bequeath to the international working-class my hope of a better world"—is exactly like the cry of the poilu in Dos Passos's callow first novel, *One Man's Initiation*—"Oh, the lies, the lies, the lies, the lies that life is smothered in! We must strike once more for freedom, for the sake of the dignity of man. Hopelessly, cynically, ruthlessly, we must rise and show at least that we are not taken in; that we are slaves but not willing slaves." From Martin Howe to Glenn Spotswood, the Dos Passos hero is the young man who fails and is broken by society, but is never taken in. Whatever else he loses—and the Dos Passos characters invariably lose, if they have ever possessed, almost everything that is life to most people—he is not taken in. Hemingway has "grace under pressure," and the drama in his work is always the inherently passionate need of life: the terrible insistence on the individual's need of survival, the drumming fear that he may not survive. Dos Passos, though he has so intense an imagination, has not Hemingway's grace, his need to make so dark and tonal a poetry of defeat; he centers everything around the inviolability of the individual, his sanctity. The separation of the individual from society in Hemingway may be irrevocable, but it is tragically felt; his cynicism can seem so flawless and dramatic only because it mocks itself. In Dos Passos that separation is organic and self-willed: the mind has made its refusal, and the fraternity that it seeks and denies in the same voice can never enter into it.

It is in this concern with the primacy of the individual, with his need to save the individual from society rather than to establish him in or over it, that one can trace the conflict that runs all through Dos Passos's work—between his estheticism and strong social interests; his profound absorption in the total operations of modern society and his overscrupulous withdrawal from all of them; the iron, satirical prose he hammered out in *U.S.A.* (a machine prose for a machine world) and the youthful, stammering lyricism that pulses under it. Constitutionally a rebel and an outsider, in much of his work up to *U.S.A.* a pale and self-conscious esthete, Dos Passos is at once the most precious of the lost-generation writers and the first of the American "technological" novelists, the first to bring the novel squarely into the Machine Age and to use its rhythms, its stock piles of tools and people, in his books.

Dos Passos has never reached the dramatic balance of Hemingway's great period, the ability to concentrate all the resources of his sensibility at one particular point. The world is always a gray horror, and it is forever coming undone; his mind is forever quarreling with itself. It is only because he has never been able to accept a mass society that he has always found so morbid a fascination in it. The modern equation cancels out to zero, everything comes undone, the heroes are always broken, and the last figure in *U.S.A.*, brooding like Dos Passos himself over that epic of failure, is a starving and homeless boy walking alone up the American highway. Oppression and inequity have to be named and protested, as the democratic conscience in Dos Passos always does go on protesting to the end. Yet what he said of Thorstein Veblen in one of the most brilliantly written biographies in *U.S.A.* is particularly true of himself: he can "never get his mouth round the essential yes." The protest is never a Socialist protest, because that will substitute one collectivity for another; nor is it poetic or religious, because Dos Passos's mind, while sensitive and brilliant in inquiry, is steeped in materialism. It is a radical protest, but it is the protest against the status quo of a mind groping for more than it can define to itself, the protest of a mind whose opposition to capitalism is no greater than his suspicion of all societies.

In Dos Passos's early work, so much of which is trivial and merely preparatory to the one important work of his career, *U.S.A.*, this conflict meant the conflict between the esthete and the world even in broadly social novels like *Three Soldiers* and *Manhattan Transfer*. But under the surface of preciosity that covers those early novels, there is always the story of John Roderigo Dos Passos, grandson of a Portuguese immigrant, and like Thorstein Veblen—whose mordant insights even more than Marx's revolutionary critique give a base in social philosophy to *U.S.A.*—an outsider. Growing up with all the advantages of upper-middle-class education and travel that his own father could provide for him, Dos Passos nevertheless could not help growing up with the sense of difference which even the sensitive grandsons of immigrants can feel in America. He went to Choate and to Harvard; he was soon to graduate into the most distinguished of all the lost generation's finishing schools, the Norton-Harjes Ambulance Service subsidized by a Morgan partner; but he was out of the main line, out just enough in his own mind to make the difference that can make men what they are.

It is not strange that Dos Passos has always felt such intimate ties with the Hispanic tradition and community, or that in his very revealing little travel book, *Rosinante to the Road Again,* he mounted Don Quixote's nag and named himself Telemachus, as if to indicate that his postwar pilgrimage in Spain was, like Telemachus's search for Ulysses, a search for his own father-principle, the continuity he needed to find in Hispania. It was in Spain and in Latin America that Dos Passos learned to prize men like the Mexican revolutionary Zapata, and the libertarian Anarchists of Spain. As his travel diaries and particularly the biographical sketches that loom over the narrative in *U.S.A.* tell us, Dos Passos's heart has always gone out to the men who are lonely and human in their rebellion, not to the victors and the politicians in the social struggle, but to the great defeated—the impractical but human Spanish Anarchists, the Veblens, the good Mexicans, the Populists and the Wobblies, the Bob La Follettes, the Jack Reeds, the Randolph Bournes, all defeated and uncontrolled to the last, most of them men distrustful of too much power, of centralization, of the glib revolutionary morality which begins with hatred and terror and believes it can end with fraternity. So even the first figure in *U.S.A.*, the itinerant Fenian McCreary, "Mac," and the last, "Vag," are essentially Wobblies and "working stiffs"; so even Mary French, the most admirable character in the whole trilogy, is a defeated Bolshevik. And it is only the defeated Bolsheviks whom Dos Passos ever really likes. The undefeated seem really to defeat themselves.

The grandson of the Portuguese immigrant was also, however, the boy who entered college, as Malcolm Cowley has pointed out, "at the beginning of a period which was later known as that of the Harvard esthetes." The intellectual atmosphere there was that of "young men who read Pater and 'The Hill of Dreams,' who argued about St. Thomas in sporting houses, and who wandered through the slums of South Boston with dull eyes for 'the long rain slanting on black walls' and eager eyes for the face of an Italian woman who, in the midst of this squalor, suggested the Virgin in Botticelli's Annunciation." Dos Passos went to the slums; and he could find the Botticelli Virgin there. The *Harvard Monthly* was publishing his first pieces: a free-verse poem, an editorial, and an essay on industrialism entitled "A Humble Protest." "Are we not," asked the young author, "like men crouching on a runaway engine? And at the same time we insensately shovel in the fuel with no thought as to where we are being taken." It was but one step from this to *One Man's Initiation,* published in England in 1920, and significantly subtitled *1917*. For this first of his two antiwar novels made no pretense to the hard-boiled realism of *Three Soldiers*. It was the very boyish and arty memoir of a young architect-poet whose chief grievance against the war, in a way, seems to have been that he could not admire the Gothic cathedrals in France for the clamor of the guns in his ears. The hero, consciously posing himself against a Europe

ravaged by war, was a pale imitation of all the pale heroes in fin-de-
siècle fiction, a hand-me-down Huysmans torn between a desire to
enter a monastery, a taste for architecture, and a need to write a
ringing manifesto for all the embittered artist-revolutionaries in the
world. "God!" exclaims Martin Howe in the trenches, "if only there
were somewhere nowadays where you could flee from all this stupidity, from all this cant of governments, and this hideous reiteration
of hatred, this strangling hatred."

By 1921, with *Three Soldiers,* the esthete had become something
more of the social novelist. The rhetorical petulance of *One Man's
Initiation* had given way to a dull, gritty hatred. No longer could
Dos Passos write a sentence such as "Like the red flame of the sunset
setting fire to opal sea and sky, the old exaltation, the old flame that
would consume to ashes all the lies in the world, the trumpet-blast
under which the walls of Jericho would fall down, stirs and broods
in the womb of his grey lassitude." He was a realist whose odyssey
of three buck privates—Fuselli from the West, Chrisfield from the
South, John Andrews the musician from New York—was an attempt
to tell in miniature the national story of the A.E.F. Yet for all the
grimness of *Three Soldiers,* the sounding in it of the characteristically terse and mocking tone of Dos Passos's later social novels, it
was essentially as flaky and self-consciously romantic as *One Man's
Initiation.* There are three protagonists in the book, but only one
hero, John Andrews; and it is his humiliation and agony in war that
finally dominate the book. It is interesting to note that in this first
important novel Dos Passos had already shown that interest in the
type, the mass as central protagonist, that would distinguish *U.S.A.;*
and certainly nothing is so good in the book as his ability to suggest
the gray anonymity, the treadmill, the repeated shocks and prob-
ings of the private's experience, the hysterical barroom jokes and
convulsive brothel loves, the boredom and weariness.

Yet it is even more significant that Dos Passos did sacrifice his inclusive design to John Andrews. For Andrews is what he cares most
for; Andrews is a sadder and older brother to Martin Howe, the shy
and esthetic and fumbling Dos Passos hero, and like the hedonists
of *1919,* he survives the war only to die—at least symbolically, at

the hands of the military police—in the peace. Where the enemy in *One Man's Initiation* was abstract, the society at war in *Three Soldiers* is a bureaucratic horror. But the war does exist still only as something oppressive to John Andrews; the artist is against the world, and when Andrews speaks out of his full heart at the end of the book, it is to say to Jeanne: "We must live very much, we who are free to make up for all the people who are still . . . bored." The artist has no place in war, as in a sense he has no place in the industrial mass society Dos Passos has not yet discovered; war seems only the last brazen cruelty of the enemy, the outrage inflicted upon those who would live bravely and be passionately free—for art. The army is the public self (Dos Passos can never accept the public self); the artist can only conceal himself in it or die by it. "This sentient body of his, full of possibilities and hopes and desires, was only a pale ghost that depended on the other self, that suffered for it and cringed for it." And the public self wins; it always will in Dos Passos. So John Andrews, who deserted to write a great orchestral poem (around the Queen of Sheba), is captured after all; and when the police take him away, the sheets of music flutter slowly into the breeze.

Thirteen years after he had completed *Three Soldiers,* Dos Passos wrote that it was a book that had looked forward to the future. For all its bitterness, he had written it as an epilogue to the war from which men in 1919 seemed to be turning to reconstruction or even revolution. "Currents of energy seemed breaking out everywhere as young guys climbed out of their uniforms . . . in every direction the countries of the world stretched out starving and angry, ready for anything turbulent and new." He himself had gone on to Spain, Telemachus looking for the father and teasing himself because he was so callow. Spain was where the old romantic castles still remained; Spain had been neutral during the war; in Spain one might even be free of the generation "to which excess is a synonym for beauty." In Spain there were the Anarchists, and tranquillity without resignation, and the kind of life that would develop a Pio Baroja, physician and baker and novelist of revolution. "It's always death," cries the friend in *Rosinante to the Road Again,* "but we must go on. . . . Many years ago I should have set out to right wrong—for no one but a man, an individual alone, can right a wrong; organization merely substitutes one wrong for another—but now. . . ." But now Telemachus is listening to Pio Baroja, whose characters, as he describes them, are so much like the characters in *Manhattan Transfer* and *U.S.A.*—"men whose nerve has failed, who live furtively on the outskirts, snatching a little joy here and there, drugging their hunger with gorgeous mirages." Baroja is a revolutionary novelist as Dos Passos only seems to be, but as Dos Passos reports Baroja's conception of the middle-class intellectual, one can see his own self-portrait:

> He has not undergone the discipline which can only come from common slavery in the industrial machine, necessary for a builder. His slavery has been an isolated slavery which has unfitted him forever from becoming truly part of a community. He can use the vast power of knowledge which training has given him only in one way. His great mission is to put the acid test to existing institutions, and to strip the veils off them.

By 1925, when he published *Manhattan Transfer,* Dos Passos had come to a critical turn in his career. He had been uprooted by the war, he had fled from the peace; but he could not resolve himself in flight. More than any other American novelist of the contemporary generation, Dos Passos was fascinated by the phenomenon of a mass society in itself; but his mind had not yet begun to study seriously the configuration of social forces, the naturalism and social history, which were to become his great subject in *U.S.A.* Like so much that he wrote up to 1930, *Manhattan Transfer* is only a preparation for *U.S.A.,* and like so many of those early works, it is a mediocre, weakly written book. He had as yet no real style of his own; he has not even in *Manhattan Transfer.* But he was reaching in that book for a style and method distinctively his own; and just as the Sacco-Vanzetti case was two years later to crystallize the antagonism to American capitalist society that is the base of *U.S.A.,* so the experimental form of *Manhattan Transfer,* its attempt to play on the shuttle of the great city's life dozens of human stories representative of the mass scene (and, for Dos Passos, the mass agony), was to lead straight into the brilliantly original technique of *U.S.A.*

Yet the achievement in style and technique of *Manhattan Transfer* is curiously inconclusive and muddy. The book seems to flicker in the gaslight of Dos Passos's own confusion. Out of the endlessly changing patterns of metropolitan life he drew an image that was collective. He was all through this period working in expressionist drama, as plays like *The Garbage Man, Airways, Inc.,* and *Fortune Heights* testify; and as in the expressionist plays of Georg Kaiser and Ernst Toller, he sketched out in his novel a tragic ballet to the accompaniment of the city's music and its mass chorus. Most significantly, he was working out a kind of doggerel prose style completely removed from his early lushness, full of the slangy rhythms he had picked up in *Three Soldiers* by reproducing soldier speech, and yet suggestive of a wry and dim poetry. This new style Dos Passos evidently owed in part to contemporary poetry, and like his trick of liquefying scenes together as if in a dream sequence and fusing words to bring out their exact tonal reverberation in the mind, to James Joyce. But what this meant in *Manhattan Transfer* was that the romantic poet, the creator and double of Martin Howe and John Andrews and the novel's Jimmy Herf, had become fascinated with a kind of mass and pictorial ugliness. The book was like a perverse esthetic geometry in which all the colors of the city's scenes were daubed together madly, and all its frames jumbled. What one saw in *Manhattan Transfer* was not the broad city pattern at all, but a wistful absorption in monstrousness. The poet-esthete still stood against the world, and rejected it completely. Characteristically even the book's hero (*U.S.A.* was to have no heroes, only symbols), Jimmy Herf, moons through it only to walk out into the dawn after a last party in Greenwich Village, bareheaded and alone, to proclaim his complete disgust with the megalopolis of which he was, as the Dos Passos poet-heroes always are, the victim.

So Dos Passos himself, though torn between what he had learned from Pio Baroja and his need to take refuge in "the esthete's cell," was ready to flee again. The conflict all through his experience be-

tween the self and the world, the conflict that he had been portray-
ing with growing irony and yet so passionately in all his works, was
coming to a head. And now the social insights he had been gather-
ing from his own personal sense of isolation, from his bitterness
against the war, from Spain, were kindled by the martyrdom of
Sacco and Vanzetti. More perhaps than any other American writer
who fought to obtain their freedom, it can be said, Dos Passos was
really educated and toughened, affected as an artist, by the long and
dreary months he spent working for them outside Charlestown
Prison. For many writers the Sacco-Vanzetti case was at most a
shock to their acquiescent liberalism or indifference; for Dos Passos
it provided immediately the catalyst (he had never been acquiescent
or indifferent) his work had needed, the catalyst that made *U.S.A.*
possible. It transformed his growingly irritable but persistently romantic obsession with the poet's struggle against the world into a
use of the class struggle as his base in art. The Sacco-Vanzetti case
gave him, in a word, the beginnings of a formal conception of society; and out of the bitter realization that this society—the society
Martin Howe had mocked, that John Andrews had been crushed
by, that Jimmy Herf had escaped—could grind two poor Italian
Anarchists to death for their opinions, came the conception of the
two nations, the two Americas, that is the scaffolding of *U.S.A.*

Dos Passos knew where he stood now: the old romantic polarity
had become a social polarity, and America lay irrevocably split in his
mind between the owners and the dispossessed, between those who
wielded the police power and the great masses of people. He began
to write *The 42nd Parallel*, the first volume in *U.S.A.*, after the
Sacco-Vanzetti case; and the trilogy itself draws to its end after Mary
French's return from their execution in *The Big Money*. The most
deeply felt writing in all of *U.S.A.* is Dos Passos's own commentary
on the Sacco-Vanzetti case in the "Camera Eye," where he speaks in
his own person, an eloquent hymn of compassion and rage that is
strikingly different from the low-toned stream-of-consciousness prose
that is usually found in the "Camera Eye" sections, and which lifts
it for a moment above the studied terseness and coldness of the
whole work:

they have clubbed us off the streets   they are stronger   they are rich   they hire and fire the politicians the newspapereditors the old judges the small men with reputations the collegepresidents the wardheelers (listen businessmen collegepresidents judges   America will not forget her betrayers) they hire the men with guns the uniforms the policecars the patrolwagons

all right you have won   you will kill the brave men our friends tonight

America our nation has been beaten by strangers who have turned our language inside out who have taken the clean words our fathers spoke and made them slimy and foul

their hired men sit on the judge's bench they sit back with their feet on the tables under the dome of the State House they are ignorant of our beliefs they have the dollars the guns the armed forces the powerplants

they have built the electricchair and hired the executioner to throw the switch

all right we are two nations

All right we are two nations. It is the two nations that compose the story of *U.S.A.* But it was the destruction of two individuals, symbolic as they were, that brought out this polarity in Dos Passos's mind, their individual martyrdom that called the book out. From first to last Dos Passos is primarily concerned with the sanctity of the individual, and the trilogy proper ends with Mary French's defeat and growing disillusionment, with the homeless boy "Vag" alone on the road. It is not Marx's two classes and Marx's optimism that speak in *U.S.A.* at the end; it is Thorstein Veblen, who like Pio Baroja could "put the acid test to existing institutions and strip the veils off them," but "couldn't get his mouth round the essential yes." And no more can Dos Passos. *U.S.A.* is a study in the history of modern society, of its social struggles and great masses; but it is a history of defeat. There are no flags for the spirit in it, and no victory save the mind's silent victory that integrity can acknowledge to itself. It is one of the saddest books ever written by an American.

Technically *U.S.A.* is one of the great achievements of the modern novel, yet what that achievement is can easily be confused with its elaborate formal structure. For the success of Dos Passos's method does not rest primarily on his schematization of the novel into four panels, four levels of American experience—the narrative proper, the "Camera Eye," the "Biographies," and the "Newsreel." That arrangement, while original enough, is the most obvious thing in the book and soon becomes the most mechanical. The book lives by its narrative style, the wonderfully concrete yet elliptical prose which bears along and winds around the life stories in the book like a conveyor belt carrying Americans through some vast Ford plant of the human spirit. *U.S.A.* is a national epic, the first great national epic of its kind in the modern American novel; and its triumph is not the pyrotechnical display that the shuttling between the various devices seems to suggest, but Dos Passos's power to weave so many different lives together in narrative. It is possible that the narrative sections would lose much of that power if they were not so craftily built into the elaborate framework of the book. But the framework holds the book together and encloses it; the narrative makes it. The "Newsreel," the "Camera Eye," and even the very vivid and often brilliant "Biographies" are meant to lie a little outside the book always; they speak with the formal and ironic voice of History. The "Newsreel" sounds the time; the "Biographies" stand above time, chanting the stories of American leaders; the "Camera Eye" moralizes shyly in a lyric stammer upon them. But the great thing about *U.S.A.* is that though it sweeps up so many human lives together and intones their waste and illusion and defeat so steadily, we seem to be swept along with them and to see each life perfectly at the moment it passes by us.

The brilliance of the structure lies therefore not so much in its external surface design as in its internal one, in the manifold rhythms of the narrative. Each of the various narrative sections has its dominant musical mode, as it were; each of the characters is encased in his characteristic prose. Thus at the very beginning of *The 42nd Parallel,* when the "Newsreel" blares in a welcome to the new century, while General Miles falls off his horse and Senator Beveridge's toast to the new imperialist America is heard, the story of Fenian McCreary, "Mac," begins with the smell of whale-oil soap in the printer's house in Middletown. That smell, the clatter of the presses, the political arguments, the muddy streets and saloons, give the tone of Mac's life from the first, as his life—Wobbly, tramp, working stiff—sounds the emergence of labor as a dominant force in the new century. So the story of Eleanor Stoddard begins with "When she was small she hated everything," a sentence that calls up the thin-lipped rebellion and superciliousness, the artiness and desperation, of her loveless life before we have gone into it. *The 42nd Parallel* is a study in youth, of the youth of the new century, the "new America," and of all the human beings who figure in it; and it is in the world of Mac's bookselling and life on freights, of Eleanor Stoddard's rebellion against her father and Janey Williams's picnic near the falls at Georgetown, of J. Ward Moorehouse's Wilmington and the railroad boarding house Charley Anderson's mother kept in North Dakota, that we move. The narrator behind his "Camera Eye" is a little boy holding to his mother's hand, listening to his father's boasts (at the end of the book he will be on his way to France); the "Newsreel" sings out the headlines and popular songs of 1900–16; the "Biographies" are of the magnates (Minor C. Keith, Carnegie), the wonder men of the new century (Steinmetz, Edison, Burbank), the rebels (Bryan, Debs, Bob La Follette, Big Bill Haywood).

We have just left the world of childhood behind us in *The 42nd Parallel,* but we can already hear the clatter of the conveyor belt pushing all these lives along. Everyone is sparring hard for position; the fences of life are going up. There is no expectancy in this youth, not even the sentimental poetry of adolescence. The "Newsreel" singing the lush ballads of 1906 already seems very far away; the "Biographies" are effigies in stone. The life in the narrative has become dominant; the endless pulsing drowns everything else out. Everything is hard, dry, and already a little outrageous. Johnny Moorehouse falls in love only to learn that the socially prominent girl whom he needs for his ambition is a whore. When Eleanor Stoddard's father announces his plan to marry again, he tells her it will be to a "Mrs. O'Toole, a widow with five children who kept a boardinghouse out Elsden way." Mac, after his bitterly hard youth, leaves the Wobblies with whom he has found comradeship and the joy of battle to marry a girl who drives him almost insane; then leaves her and is thrown into the Mexican revolutions of the period. Janey Williams's life has already taken on the gray color of the offices in which she will spend her life. There are no refuges in this world, no evasions, and above all no second starts. The clamps have been laid down early, and for all time.

Yet we can feel the toneless terror of all these lives, the oppression and joylessness that seem to beat down upon us from the first, only because every narrative section is so concrete and every sentence, as Delmore Schwartz pointed out, "can expand in the reader's mind to include a whole context of experience." *U.S.A.* is perhaps the first great naturalistic novel that is primarily a triumph of style. Everything that lives in the book is wound up on the spool of that style; from the fragments of popular songs in the "Newsreel" and the clean verse structure of the "Biographies" down to the pounding beat of the narrative, the book seems to be propelled by one dynamic rhythm. The Dos Passos prose, once so uncertain and self-conscious, has here been whittled down to a sharpness that can kill; but it has by no means lost its old wistful rhetoric in *U.S.A.*, which is particularly conspicuous in the impressionist "Camera Eye" sections, and generally gives a kind of secret and mischievous color to the severely reportorial prose. Scrubby, slangy, with a kind of grim straightforwardness, it is the style of a very cunning artisan who seems to be working in these human materials as another might work in stone or wood—forever carving away, forever whittling, but never without subtle turns and a loving sense of design. It is never a "distinguished" style, beautiful in its own right; never as prismatic as Fitzgerald's or as delicately molded as Hemingway's, and there is always something fundamentally mechanical about it. But it is the style Dos Passos needs to turn the motor of the conveyor belt; it is the reportorial and satiric style needed to push along and circumscribe all these lives. With *The 42nd Parallel* we have entered into a machine world in which the rhythm of the machine has become the primal beat of all the people in it; and Dos Passos's hard, lean, mocking prose, forever sounding that beat, calling them to their deaths, has become the supreme expression of his conception of them.

Perhaps nowhere in the trilogy, save in the descending spiral of Charley Anderson's life in the first half of *The Big Money*, is Dos Passos's use of symbolic rhythm so brilliant as in the story of Joe Williams in *1919*. For Joe, Janey Williams's sailor brother, is the leading protagonist of the war and the early postwar period, as J. Ward Moorehouse's ambitiousness marked the pattern of *The 42nd Parallel*. Joe's endless shuttling between the continents on rotting freighters has become the migration and rootlessness of the young American generation whom we saw growing up in *The 42nd Parallel*; and the growing stupor and meaninglessness of his life became the leit-motif of the waste and death that hold everyone in the book as in a ghostly vise. The theme of death, of the false optimism immediately after the Armistice, are sounded immediately by the narrator behind his "Camera Eye" reporting the death of his mother and the notation on the coming of peace—"tomorrow I hoped would be the first day of the first month of the first year." The "Biographies" are all studies in death and defeat, from Randolph Bourne to Wesley Everest, mutilated and lynched after the Centralia shootings in Washington in 1919; from the prose poem commemorating the dozens of lives the Unknown Soldier might have led to the death's-head portrait of J. P. Morgan ("Wars and panics on the stock exchange,/ machinegunfire and arson/ . . . starvation, lice, cholera and typhus"). The "Camera Eye" can detect only "the almond smell of high explosives sending singing éclats through the sweetish puking grandiloquence of the rotting dead." And sounding its steady beat under the public surface of war is the story of Joe Williams hurled between the continents—Joe, the supreme Dos Passos cipher and victim and symbol, suffering his life with dumb unconsciousness of how outrageous his life is, and continually loaded and dropped from one ship to another like a piece of cargo.

> Twentyfive days at sea on the steamer *Argyle,* Glasgow, Captain Thompson, loaded with hides, chipping rust, daubing red lead on steel plates that were sizzling hot griddles in the sun, painting the stack from dawn to dark, pitching and rolling in the heavy dirty

swell, bedbugs in the bunks in the stinking focastle, slumgullion for grub, with potatoes full of eyes and mouldy beans.

All through *1919* one can hear death being sounded. Every life in it, even J. Ward Moorehouse's, has become a corrosion, a slow descent. Richard Ellsworth Savage goes back on his early idealism and becomes a cynical but willing abetter in Moorehouse's schemes. Eveline Hutchins and Eleanor Stoddard lose all their genteel pretense to art and grapple for Moorehouse's favor. "Daughter," the Texas girl Savage has betrayed, falls to her death in an airplane. Even Ben Compton, the New York radical, soon finds himself rotting away in prison. The war for almost all of them has become an endless round of drink and travel; they have brought nothing to it and learned nothing from it save a growing consciousness of their futility. And when they all slip into the twenties and the boom with *The Big Money,* the story of Charley Anderson's precipitate rise and fall becomes the last mad parable of their existence, a carnival of greed and corruption. Beginning with Dick Savage's life on ambulances and trains over France and Italy in *1919,* the pace of the trilogy has become faster and faster; now, as the war world empties into the pleasure world of *The Big Money*—New York and Detroit, Hollywood and Miami at the height of the boom—it has become a death ride. There is money in the air, money and power for Charley Anderson and Margo Dowling and Dick Savage; but as they come closer to this material triumph, their American dream, the machine has begun to spin them too rapidly. Charley Anderson can kiss the bright new century notes in his wallet, Margo can rise higher and higher in Hollywood, Dick Savage, having sold out completely, can enjoy his power at the hands of J. Ward Moorehouse; the machine has begun to strangle them; there is no joy here for anyone. All through *The Big Money* we wait for the balloon to collapse, for the death cry we hear in that last drunken drive of Charley Anderson's and his smashup.

What Waldo Frank said of Mencken is particularly relevant to Dos Passos: he brings energy to despair. Not merely does the writing in the trilogy become richer and firmer as the characters descend into the pit, but Dos Passos himself seems so imbued with an almost mystical conviction of failure that he rises to new heights in those last sections of *The Big Money* which depict the last futile efforts of the liberals and radicals to save Sacco and Vanzetti, and their later internecine quarrels. The most moving scene in all of *U.S.A.* is the scene in which Mary French, the only counterpoise to the selfishness of the other characters in *The Big Money,* becomes so exhausted by her labors for Sacco and Vanzetti that when she goes to bed she dreams that her whole world is forever coming apart, that she is climbing up a shaky hillside "among black guttedlooking houses pitching at crazy angles where steelworkers lived" and being thrown back. The conflicting hopes of Mary French, who wanted Socialism, and of Charley Anderson, who wanted the big money, have brought two different kinds of failure; but it is failure that broods over them and over everyone else in *U.S.A.* in the end—over the pompous fakes like J. Ward Moorehouse, the radicals like Ben Compton, the grasping little animals like Eleanor Stoddard and Eveline Hutchins, the opportunists like Richard Ellsworth Savage. The two survivors are Margo Dowling, supreme for the moment in Hollywood, and the homeless boy "Vag," who stands alone on the Lincoln Highway, gazing up at the transcontinental plane above winging its way west, the plane full of solid and well-fed citizens glittering in the American sun, the American dream. *All right we are two nations.* And like the scaffolding of hell in *The Divine Comedy,* they are frozen into eternity; for Dos Passos there is nothing else, save the integrity of the camera eye that must see this truth and report it, the integrity and sanctity of the individual locked up in the machine world of modern society.

With *The Big Money,* published at the height of the nineteen-thirties, the story of the twenties comes to a close; but even more does it bring the story of the lost generation to a close, that generation which has stood at the peak of modern time in America as no other has. Here in *U.S.A.,* in the most ambitious of all its works, is its measure of the national life, its conception of history—and it is a history of struggle that is vain, of failure that is irrevocable, and of final despair. There is strength in *U.S.A.,* Dos Passos's own strength, the strength of the craft that can weld so many lives together and make them live so intensely before us as they pass. But for the rest it is a brilliant hecatomb, and one of the coldest and most mechanical of tragic novels. By the time we have come to the end of *U.S.A.* we begin to feel what Edmund Wilson could detect in Dos Passos before it appeared, that "his disapproval of capitalistic society becomes a distaste for all the human beings who compose it." The protest, the lost-generation "I," has taken all of them into his vision; he has given us his truth. Yet if it intones anything affirmative in the end, it is the pronouncement of young Orestes Brownson— "There is no such thing as reforming the mass without reforming the individuals who compose it." It is this conviction, rising to a bitter crescendo in *Adventures of a Young Man,* this unyielding protest against modern society on the part of a writer who has now turned back to the roots of "our storybook democracy" in works like *The Ground We Stand On* and his projected life of Thomas Jefferson, that separates Dos Passos from so many of the social novelists who follow after him in the thirties. Where he speaks of sanctity, they speak of survival; where he lives by the truth of the camera eye, they live *in* the vortex of that society which Does Passos has always been able to measure, with hatred but not in panic, from the outside. Dos Passos is the first of the new naturalists, and *U.S.A.* is the dominant social novel of the thirties; but it is not merely a vanished social period that it commemorates: it is an individualism, a protestantism, a power of personal disassociation, that seem almost to speak from another world.

Dos Passos, Fitzgerald, and History

by John William Ward

What I wish to do, finally, is to raise the matter of the relation of literature to history, but rather than confront that general problem in abstract terms let me begin with two particular literary events, one in Scott Fitzgerald's *The Great Gatsby*, the other in John Dos Passos's *USA*. The moment in *The Great Gatsby* is that lyrical conclusion when Nick Carraway, the narrator, through whose intelligence we see the action of the book, comes to Gatsby's house and stands there and ruminates on the meaning of what has happened:

> Most of the big shore places were closed now and there were hardly any lights except the shadowy, moving glow of a ferryboat across the Sound. And as the moon rose higher the inessential houses began to melt away until gradually I became aware of the old island here that flowered once for Dutch sailors' eyes—a fresh, green breast of the new world. Its vanished trees, the trees that had made way for Gatsby's house, had once pandered in whispers to the last and greatest of all human dreams; for a transitory enchanted moment man must have held his breath in the presence of this continent, compelled into an aesthetic contemplation he neither understood nor desired, face to face for the last time in history with something commensurate to his capacity for wonder.
>
> And as I sat there brooding on the old, unknown world, I thought of Gatsby's wonder when he first picked out the green light at the end of Daisy's dock. He had come a long way to this blue lawn, and

his dream must have seemed so close that he could hardly fail to grasp it. He did not know that it was already behind him, somewhere back in that vast obscurity beyond the city, where the dark fields of the republic rolled on under the night.

Nick asks us at this point to identify Gatsby's story with the whole story of the discovery and the meaning of America. Gatsby's story and the meaning of his failure are somehow linked to the meaning of the American experience. The critical matter is that it is the imagery of greenness which connects Gatsby's story with the American story. Greenness becomes the physical symbol of an enchanted moment, a transitory moment when man had something commensurate to his capacity for wonder. For the discoverers, it points to a fresh and open new world; for Gatsby, to Daisy. For Nick, and for us, it points to the past, the loss of an ideal, of a vanished dream. If Jay Gatsby has failed in the pursuit of some ideal vision, so (we are made to feel) has America.

The second literary episode I would like to use is the Sacco-Vanzetti sequence in *The Big Money* at Camera Eye 49 and 50, where (in a stream of consciousness) the narrator ruminates, like Nick, on the meaning of the action.

The Camera Eye (49)

walking from Plymouth to North Plymouth through the raw air of Massachusetts Bay at each step a small cold squudge through the sole of one shoe

looking out past the gray frame houses under the robin'segg April sky across the white dories anchored in the bottleclear shallows across the yellow sandbars and the slaty bay ruffling to blue to the eastward

this is where the immigrants landed the roundheads the sackers of castles the kingkillers haters of oppression this is where they stood in a cluster after landing from the crowded ship that stank of bilge on the beach that belonged to no one between the ocean that belonged to no one and the enormous forest that belonged to no one that stretched over the hills where the deertracks were up the green rivervalleys where the redskins grew their tall corn in patches forever into the incredible west

for threehundred years the immigrants toiled into the west

and now today

walking from Plymouth to North Plymouth suddenly round a bend
in the road beyond a little pond and yellowtwigged willows hazy with
green you see the Cordage   huge sheds and buildings companyhouses
all the same size all grimed the same color a great square chimney
long roofs sharp ranked squares and oblongs cutting off the sea in
Plymouth Cordage   this is where another immigrant worked hater of
oppression who wanted a world unfenced

Another immigrant is, of course, Bart Vanzetti, an Italian fishpeddler, yet a "founder" of Massachusetts because he believes in
the "old" words grown slimy in the mouths of lawyers and college
presidents and judges. What happens to language and the meaning
of words is important for an understanding of *USA,* but for the
moment I want to stress the landscape of defeat and betrayal. In
the next Camera Eye, the "I" of the novel, the consciousness which
moves through the book, accepts defeat.

Camera Eye (50)

all right we are two nations

America our nation has been beaten by strangers who have bought
the laws and fenced off the meadows and cut down the woods for
pulp and turned our pleasant cities into slums and sweated the
wealth out of our people and when they want to they hire the executioner to throw the switch

In *USA,* just as in *The Great Gatsby,* the betrayal of the meaning
of America, the corruption of words and values, is dramatized by the
movement from "a world unfenced" to the monotonous, ranked
squares of the factory which shut one off from nature. Just as we are
asked by Fitzgerald to identify Gatsby's personal dream with the historical promise of a green new world, so Dos Passos asks us to feel
the defeat of Sacco and Vanzetti as the defeat of America, again
linked to the violation of nature, the fencing of the meadows and
the closing of the openness of the continent. Both *The Great Gatsby*
and *USA* are sad books, books of defeat. *USA* is not only that; it is, I
think, the coldest, most mercilessly despairing book in our literature. As far apart as they are in other ways, however, both books at

climactic moments, project the sense of loss, of failure, of betrayal, through the violation of greenness, of meadows, of open, inviting, unravaged nature.

But so much has been written about *The Great Gatsby,* let me speak more to *USA.*

USA is generally placed in the tradition of naturalism in our literature, but naturalism is one of those large abstractions which threatens to conceal reality rather than disclose it or define it. So, let me say that, for me, literary naturalism is not a technique or a style, it is a point of view, a definition of the author's perspective on his subject matter. It implies some species of determinism; the human beings in the action are determined by some force outside their own personalities, whether that force be God, or biology, or the instincts of sex, or class in the Marxist version. In the United States, industrialism and the sudden passage into an urban world led in our literature to the stress on the overpowering and mastering force of the environment which reduces the individual to a function of a power, the dynamics of which lie outside the determination of human personality.

Let me emphasize a literary problem in naturalism. The subject of a work of fiction written from a naturalistic premise is that the individual does not count. You cannot have a hero in the traditional sense. You cannot have a hero who dominates the action because the whole point of naturalistic fiction is that the environment, or force, however defined, transcends and dominates the individual. The environment, in other words, is your subject; individual human beings, your characters, become simply shadows of environmental force. The point is simple and obvious enough, but the American writer, responding to a sense of the fatality of society, who wanted to write about society itself, the whole complex structure of relationships rather than about a single human being—a hero—had no developed tradition at hand to assist him in the technical problem of organizing his fiction.

Let me make the general specific by drawing your attention to two books, William Dean Howells' *A Hazard of New Fortunes*

(1890) and Henry Blake Fuller's *The Cliff-Dwellers* (1893), which are attempts to solve the problem. I say attempts because both fail and it was left, I think, to Dos Passos to succeed, but Howells and Fuller are instructive because of what they fumblingly tried to do.

As one stands back from *A Hazard of New Fortunes,* its scope, when we think of Howells' other fiction, is astonishingly large. Among its many characters, there is a representative of nearly every shade of opinion in the America of its time: we find a *fin de siecle,* alienated artist, a speculating capitalist, a brash entrepreneur in the new field of mass journalism, a courtly and reactionary southern agrarian, a German anarchist, an idealistic representative of the social gospel movement, and many more. Clearly what Howells wants to do is to bring together a variety of figures, representing a variety of responses to the conditions of industrial society, and make the interplay of these figures his subject. But the only way Howells could imagine bringing this off was by the device of a literary magazine whose various contributors provide the spectrum of characters we discover.

Although there are strikes and violence in the book, though we know Dryfoos spends his days at the Stock Exchange, and though Basil March takes walks through the ghastly slums of New York, all this is rather off-stage. A literary magazine was closer to Howells' personal experience, but the device does not fit his purpose. Further, Howells' imagination did not reach beyond the sentimental, middle-class love story as a way of organizing his fiction and a number of these provide the dynamics of his plot rather than the apparent subject-matter, the way in which a number of individuals are functionally related to the anonymous and controlling forces of society.

Henry Blake Fuller's novel, *The Cliff-Dwellers,* is a much bolder attempt than Howells'. Fuller seized upon the modern expression of the complexity of a great city, William LeBaron Jenney's Home Insurance Building, our first skyscraper. With one masterful stroke, Fuller cut through the problem of how to write a novel about society itself rather than about the self in society, finding his controlling image in the anonymous forces of the economy embodied in a soaring office building whose occupants are related one to another only through the nexus of institutional roles in a complex economy.

The Cliff-Dwellers fails to become a fully successful book because Fuller is unable to manage his structural device. Despite his assertion that he will not wander far or often from inside his building, Clifton, by the sixth chapter he begins to wander away from what should have remained his controlling strategy and by the end of the novel we have spent more pages away from Clifton than in it. Like Howells', his book becomes a love-story, the dominant convention for the organization of the novel in American fiction unless one shipped aboard a whaler or lit out on a raft.

We can now better appreciate what Howells and Fuller were trying to do, that is, to create a structural device for a novel about society, because we can look back at their problem from the vantage point of the novel which solved the technical problem by a brilliant *tour de force*, John Dos Passos's *USA*. *USA* is, as I have said already, an icy, despairing book and it has been criticized because it presents no character with whom we can identify. The observation is a valid one but used for a mistaken conclusion. There are no people in the book, only automata walking stiffly to the beat of Dos Passos's despair. But the point of the novel, as we like to say, is that there are no individuals in American society. Dos Passos's "hero" is USA, that monstrous abstraction, Society itself. Society is the hero—or the villain—of the piece. In Dos Passos's vision, society has become depersonalized and abstract and there are no human beings, no human relations, in it. The style, as Alfred Kazin put it, is like some "conveyor belt carrying Americans through some vast Ford plant of the human spirit." As if on feeder lines in an assembly plant, lives connect one with another, but no human connection is made. We have the staccato juxtaposition of snatches of songs and headlines, historical figures and fictional characters, all observed by the passive eye of the camera, all making a bitter montage of nothingness.

Dos Passos is a difficult man to talk about. In 1932, he was one of those who signed a public statement supporting the presidential candidacy of William Z. Foster, the Communist candidate for President; twenty years later, in 1952, he supported Robert A. Taft against Eisenhower for the Republican nomination and he now writes for Mr. Buckley's *National Review*. The shift from left to right may look contradictory, but I think is not. Dos Passos is a man always opposed to power. He saw power in the hands of capitalistic businessmen in the 30s and was, therefore, on the radical left; he sees power today in the hands of liberal intellectuals, allied with labor, and is now on the conservative right. I would, of course, stress the fact that Dos Passos is responding to his own sense of where power lies in our society; we can make sense out of his position, but to accept his position would require an analysis into the accuracy of his location of power. But Dos Passos has always been a negative function of power; that is, one finds him always at the opposite pole of where he conceives power to be. In this sense, he is more an anarchist, and always was, than a socialist or a conservative.

What Dos Passos achieved in *USA* was the creation of a form appropriate to the theme of the overwhelming, impersonal force of society, a structure which would carry the meaning of the primacy of society and make the anonymous processes of society the very stuff of a fictional world. As an aside, I might say that if the student of American culture, or American civilization, assumes that there is a relationship between literature and history, he must take that assumption as seriously as it deserves and examine the way in which history enters not just the overt subject matter of literature but is there in language, imagery and, to penetrate to the heart of the matter, the very ordering of the literary object, its very structure.

The ultimate despair we confront in *USA* relates closely to what happens to language in the book. From the preface where the voice of the Camera Eye sections first identifies the meaning of America with American speech and the meaning of words, there is a constant concern, dramatically as well as explicitly, with the corruption of language. As we have seen, the betrayal of the promise of America is that words have grown slimy in the mouths of the ruling classes who have perverted old ideals. At the end of *The Big Money*, coming appropriately after William Randolph Hearst, is Richard Ellsworth Savage, the advertising man, corrupted like everyone else by the big money, who creates a campaign to sell the quack nostrums of a patent medicine fraud and to fend off pure food and drug legislation by appealing to American individualism and self-reliance and self-help. The meaning of America has been lost because all the words have been turned inside out. The last Camera Eye section ends before the biography of Insull and one has to see the page to catch the connection:

> we have only words against
>
> ### Power Superpower

Not only have words lost their meaning, they have lost their efficacy. They prove incapable of stinging people into awareness. Power Superpower finally overwhelms even the language which creates the identity of America and if Dos Passos could say "we stand defeated," the defeat was particularly keen for the writer, the man who depends on words and his belief in the efficacy of language to sustain his personal identity. I would even speculate wildly and suggest that the vision of society Dos Passos presents in *USA* was a defeat for him personally and that is perhaps why he seems, to me at least, less estimable a writer after *USA* than before it. He had ceased to believe in the power of words.

Dos Passos comes to the same conclusion as Fitzgerald. The meaning of America, its initial promise, has been lost as Americans have gone whoring after false gods. The potentiality of America, the possibility of creating the good society, has been lost as Americans have fastened their ambitions on some meretricious goal, Daisy or the Big Money. Not only do both see a perversion of the ideal meaning of America, both associate that ideal with greenness and meadows and the vast fields of the republic and place the historical possibility of realizing that ideal somewhere in the past, in some irrecoverable moment whose memory haunts the meaninglessness of a debased and sordid present. As I said at the outset, both are sad books, one a mournful threnody, the other outraged despair.

Time in Dos Passos

by Claude-Edmonde Magny

The special technique of *The Big Money* encompasses an entire, implicit metaphysic—the challenge of Being. It is important for another reason, too: thanks to this technique, Dos Passos's trilogy has a temporal structure. The several individual stories composing the trilogy, which are what one is first aware of, are not only different shots of a single reality but moments within a single development. This single development transcends each of them and exists only by virtue of the complex design they all form. It is possible to put them end to end and demonstrate their continuity; the occasional use of flashbacks when the author wants to present the past of a newly introduced character is no more frequent than it is in the movies. The nonnovelistic elements that frame the stories—the Newsreels, the Camera Eyes, the lyrical biographies—are thus seen to have a very important "linking" function: they assure the cosmic as well as the psychological continuity of the narrative. Because of them, the impersonal reality that is the subject of the book—the year 1919 or the economic inflation of the twenties—can unfold without interruption, independent of the individual consciousnesses in which it is embodied, and preserve the mythic quality Dos Passos wanted to achieve. They are like movie background music, which nobody listens to but everybody hears, and which prepares our subconscious for the images to come.

The Newsreels in particular have taken on the major role of the

"Time in Dos Passos." From *The Age of the American Novel: The Film Aesthetic of Fiction Between the Two Wars* by Claude-Edmonde Magny. Translated by Eleanor Hochman. © 1972 by Frederick Ungar Publishing Co., Inc. Reprinted by permission.

narrative to measure the rhythm of time, to give us the uninter-
rupted sound that the film of life makes as it unrolls and winds off
the reel behind the scenes. The Newsreels give us the unfolding
world events that will have repercussions on the individual destinies
of the characters. For example, J. Ward Moorehouse's story before
and after his second marriage is cut in two not so much because
of the marriage itself—which in no way interrupts a personal, emotional, and professional continuity—but because war is declared
in Europe during his honeymoon. The war does not affect the
characters' lives immediately, but it is destined to do so soon. Consequently, just as in Wagner's *Tristan and Isolde* the theme of
Isolde's death is announced by a drum in the prelude long before
it is taken up officially by the entire orchestra, so the "theme of
war" is first presented longitudinally in the nonnovelistic elements of the book: a Newsreel filled with such headlines as "CZAR
LOSES PATIENCE WITH AUSTRIA," "GENERAL WAR NEAR," "ASSASSIN SLAYS
DEPUTY JUARES"; a biography of "Andrew Carnegie, Prince of
Peace"; and a Camera Eye that appears to be the interior mono-
logue of an English sailor. Then the narrative resumes. Further
on, America's entry into the war is announced through a Camera
Eye—the interior monologue of a couple (or a group) of New
York leftist intellectuals—and a Newsreel punctuated by the re-
frain "It's a long way to Tipperary" and including headlines like
"JOFFRE ASKS TROOPS NOW."

Similarly, in *The Big Money*, the biography of Rudolph Valentino—symbol of the handsome young man who has made it, of the
gigolo elevated by the movies to the stature of a myth that has
become a reality in the collective consciousness—is interpolated into
the story at the moment when Margo Dowling leaves for Cuba
with her gigolo husband. The biography itself is introduced by the
last news item in the preceding Newsreel: "Rudolph Valentino,
noted screen star, collapsed suddenly yesterday in his apartment at
the Hotel Ambassador. Several hours later he underwent . . ." At
this moment, just as on the radio, the voice suddenly changes and
a new speaker "fades in" by announcing, in a completely different
tone: "Adagio Dancer, The nineteenyearold son of a veterinary in

Castellaneta . . ." And during all this time the story of Margo (and through her of an entire epoch) is going on uninterruptedly, though because of the novel's aesthetic we are only able to apprehend fragments of it.

Then a parenthesis begins—the story of Charley Anderson—followed by a new Newsreel and then by a Camera Eye that is the collective monologue of emigrants leaving for Havana, which brings us back to Margo's story. When Charley leaves for Detroit, where he will join a big airplane company and marry—in other words, where he will begin the series of adventures that will lead him to success, to his meeting with Margo, then to ruin and land speculations in Miami—we get a biography of the Wright brothers, aviation pioneers; a verse of "Valencia" and other songs evoking the charm of the South; a fragment of a speech by someone who has made a fortune in Miami; an excerpt from a brochure about installment buying; and so forth. The major events of Charley's life are prefigured in the evolution of society as a whole, which makes these events possible and determines their nature. His destiny is so little of his own making that it can be foretold and prophesied. Dos Passos's characters do not have their own inner rhythm; its place is taken by the objective, mechanical rhythm of social facts, which replace at every moment the personal time, the "lived time," that Charley, Margo, and Mary French are incapable of possessing. It is social time, external time, that will carry them along in its inexorable unfolding.

One can now begin to see the profound connection at the heart of *U.S.A.* between the narrative technique of the stories and the objective elements that frame them. It is *necessary* that Dos Passos's characters have no positive inner existence, that they are not in the least masters of their fate, that they be equally incapable of controlling what happens to them and how they feel about it, that they marry for who knows what reason (Charley's marriage to Gladys and Margo's to Tony are from this point of view symbolic), and that they succeed or fail depending only upon whether they are being carried forward by the tide or left abandoned by it. And all of this is true even when, like Mary French, they *want* to give their lives a sense or meaning—by, for example, social action or self-sacrifice. Two of Dos Passos's later novels, *Adventures of a Young Man* and *Number One,* present us with a diptych of two equally absurd fates—that of Glenn Spotswood, martyr to the cause of the proletariat, and that of his brother Tyler, opportunist and dipsomaniac, the yes-man and tool of Chuck Crawford, the despicable boss of a Southern state, until Crawford decides to abandon him.

In modern society neither self-sacrifice nor ambition permits a man to be "captain of his soul, master of his fate," as the Victorian poets like Kipling or Henley had too naïvely hoped. And if Dos Passos has chosen to recount his characters' lives in that terrible preterit that *deadens* events as soon as they are so described to us; if he gives us their feelings and their states of consciousness by means of a third-person pseudo-inner monologue filled with clichés, adulterants that almost invariably come from a too-obvious hypocrisy, lacking every kind of reaction normal to an authentic and spontaneous life except for the lowest biological responses; if, thanks to the diabolic magic of his style, he thus pares modern man down to the bone to show him in his misery, his nakedness, his basic nothingness; if he does all these things, it is to prepare for the appearance, the display, the *epiphaneia,* of the major character of his book—Time: the inexorable and monstrous time of contemporary capitalist society as it incoherently unwinds in Newsreels; the time that elevates and casts down Margo, Charley, and Mary, with neither discernment nor justice, and rules over the empty consciousnesses it invades and tyrannizes.

"Time," says Schelling somewhere, "is the bad conscience of all barren metaphysics." It would not be at all arbitrary (or at least no more than it is to set forth any proposition) to begin to formulate an aesthetic of the novel by saying that Time is the main character of the novel; that the novel is the literary genre on which has devolved the task of exploring and explicating every aspect and every dimension of Time; and that the novel's current popularity and triumph is quite likely at least partly due to the unhappiness

of the modern consciousness, one that has fallen away from its relationship with eternity—which it had successfully retained until
the Renaissance—and is now wounded by a traumatism of Time,
the presence of which is felt in most of the great contemporary
novels from Faulkner to Virginia Woolf. One of the functions of
criticism would then be to bring this to light and analyze it, to
expose the wound if a thoroughgoing cure is shown to be impossible.

Within a dialectic of Time, the short story corresponds to the
instant. An essentially impressionistic genre, it is—from Mérimée
to Katherine Anne Porter and from the calm garden of Balzac's
Secrets de la Princesse de Cadignan (*A Princess's Secrets*) to those
short stories of Faulkner through which a tumultuous storm sweeps
—an incision at a specific instant. To the novel, on the other hand,
belongs the third dimension—the opaque density of duration that
is alone capable of integrating the two other dimensions. Obviously, this does not mean that the author has to show a character
grow from birth to old age: the objective duration of the events
he relates does not have to exceed the twenty-four hours of classical
tragedy. Joyce's *Ulysses* and Virginia Woolf's *Mrs. Dalloway* are
unquestionably the most famous (and the most deliberate) examples; a less well-known one is Louis Guilloux's *Le Sang noir.*
And, of course, there is also Sterne's *Tristram Shandy,* which only
manages to cover the first three days of the hero's life in its several
hundred pages. But no one will be misled by appearances. The
true time of the novel, its normal time, the time most often en-
countered (the very function of the genre seems to be to exploit
it literarily), is what Bergson, in one of those simple and superficial
views so characteristic of him, called "lived time." One senses this
"lived time" in George Eliot's *Mill on the Floss,* in Balzac, in
Meredith (to say nothing of in Rosamund Lehmann). And this
"lived time" is what is lacking in Zola (but not in the Maupassant
of *Une Vie*), and so ostentatiously present in Proust.

What makes Dos Passos stand out from other novelists is undoubtedly that the characteristic time of his novels does not, to
the slightest degree, have this organic rhythm, the dense continuity

of living tissue. His characters move within "dead time"—or rather "deadened time"—with neither spurts nor continuity, where each instant comes to the fore only to be immediately replunged into nothingness. An atomic time, like that of a Cartesian universe no longer at every instant supported by continuous creation, God having defaulted once and for all. But the discontinuity is only in the detail, in the psychological awareness of the characters. If the five hundred pages of *The Big Money* are read without interruption, the reader, far from having an impression of perpetual rupture, of atomism (which would seem the inevitable result of the purposeful dislocation of the story and its multiplicity of perspectives), feels rather as if he is being carried along by a swift current. This is because the psychological time within which the characters' states of consciousness, and their acts, unfold—and the essence of which is fragmentation—is not Dos Passos's real or basic time.

His true time is the time of Society—objective, inexorable, and spatialized. The hidden mainspring of *U.S.A.* is this implacable and regular machine rhythm, already evident in *Manhattan Transfer*. The powerful impetus that carries us through these three volumes for 1500 pages is the thumping of the locomotive, the regular "chug-chug" of a ship's boilers, the whir of a taxi motor in front of a building, or the relentless circuits of those moving headlines around the big newspaper buildings—their hallucinating monotony hypnotizing the crowd, causing the stock market crash, and provoking a rash of Wall Street suicides whose repercussions would eventually reach the Scandinavian farmers of Minnesota and the plantation population of South Carolina. The inexorable pulsation at the heart of Dos Passos's work is that of the basic, regular rhythm of the transmission belt in the heart of a factory—invisible, omnipresent, all-powerful. The rhythm of the modern world itself.

It is now possible to understand its implacability, its indifference, its unpredictability—greater by far than that of classical fatality (Dike, Themis, Ananke, and Moira), which the Greeks dared not call by one name and of which it is the contemporary form. Incapable of being accelerated or slowed down by men's will or their technique (which can influence everything but Time and which is the master only of details), Time obeys its own laws, which are known to no one else—not bankers, industrialists, or capitalists (especially not capitalists); not statesmen or economists; not Ford, Insull, Hearst (especially not Hearst), or Veblen, the old man with the heavy walk who "reels off, in a buzzing hum of sarcastic and subtle phrases, the logical and ineluctable rope of daily facts with which society will hang itself." It is what defeats Insull, by means of the bankers; Ford, by means of the economic depression and the failure of the installment-buying system; Valentino, by means of a sudden and mysterious gastritis. It is the mechanical divinity—implacable as only gears can be—that pulverizes individual destinies as soon as they slow down or speed up, as soon as the individual's rhythm is no longer in accord with the regular beat, inflexible as Fate, which is Time's own rhythm.

In this sense, the most typical evolution is that of Charley Anderson, whose life rhythm speeds up—with drink, women, the excitement of business, the exhilaration of speed, money, and success—to the point where he "goes faster than the music." It is as if he has received from Time an impulse so strong that it unhinges him, makes him speculate too daringly, drink too much, and lose his money until he arrives at the final, deeply symbolic catastrophe,[1] when, while driving his car at top speed while drunk, he is crushed by the train he has tried to pass. One cannot win a race against time any more than against light.

With this vision of Time as the monstrous divinity ensconced at the heart of the modern world, we have reached the very center of Dos Passos's work. Because of its outward diversity, this work seems, at first, to be iridescent and sparkling, but like every great work, it is essentially monotonous and almost obsessional. The inexorable fate that crushes John Andrews in *The Three Soldiers*; that, in *Manhattan Transfer,* causes Stan Emery to die a miserable death, Jimmy Herf to slowly disintegrate, and Ellen Oglethorpe

---

[1] Actually, all fates in Dos Passos are symbolic. Another example is the fate of the errant sailor Joe Williams, tossed about from cargo to cargo, like the Flying Dutchman, throughout the entire war.

to take refuge in a rich marriage; that has Glenn Spotswood taken prisoner by Spanish Loyalists in *Adventures of a Young Man* and that crushes his brother Tyler—this fate is always the same goddess in different disguises, the same one that alternately exalts and casts down the characters of *U.S.A.*, that turns the cameras with the toc-toc of a coffee grinder or a machinegun, that sweeps Woodrow Wilson, Fred Taylor, and Isadora Duncan toward their varied and futile destinies.

Here we touch upon the central intuition at the heart of every profoundly original work, an intuition that the writer has had to use every resource of his art, every bit of his life itself, to communicate to us. The compensation for our attentive reading, abstract reflection, and critical meditation is the abrupt, direct, and incandescent apprehension that suddenly brings us face to face with what Henry James called "the figure in the carpet"—the profound and yet obvious secret that the artist (and this is both his servitude and his grandeur) was not able to give us except through the chaotic procession of numerous, sensually apprehendable appearances that constitute the texture of his work.

This is the justification for the outward complexity of Dos Passos's trilogy, a work that runs the risk of disconcerting, if not actually rebuffing, the reader. The author most certainly could not have communicated his intuition of an implacable, mechanistic, and socialized Time that is the sole regulator of the world by means of a simple narrative about the lives of his characters. He had to illumine them, clarifying the orientation (without which they would simply have appeared as chaotic) by framing them with objective elements, historic landmarks, dates as impersonal as those on a calendar, taken from exactly the same web of external and indifferent time within which individual destinies are unwinding. Regardless of how strange it may seem at first reading, the technique used by the author of *U.S.A.* is no more the byzantine refinement of a writer eager to proclaim his originality and somehow attract the attention of a blasé public than was that of Joyce in *Ulysses* or the deliberately obscure narration of Faulkner. It was without doubt the only means by which he could achieve his end.

One question remains: Is Dos Passos's desired effect immediately and truly achieved through these formal innovations to which he had recourse, or is the significance of his work only discerned after critical analysis? In other words, is the technique of *U.S.A.* important because of its immediate efficacy, or will it pass into literary history as an artistic curiosity, an unsuccessful example—instructive by its very failure—of what human ambition and ingenuity have aimed at?

Here the critic must invoke his personal experience and become just another reader. I thus confess to having long ignored the non-novelistic elements (and their ultimate significance) of the first two volumes of *U.S.A.* except for a few of the biographies; to having deliberately skipped over them to get on with the story; to having frequently been annoyed by them, especially by the Camera Eyes and the Newsreels, which upset me just as the bits of newspapers the surrealists integrated into their collages did; and even to having sometimes treated *1919* as I was later to treat *Les Hommes de bonne volonté,* foraging through the volumes, like a child picking all the raisins out of the pudding, for the adventures of the characters I liked best—well punished, to be sure, when I realized that important things had happened to those preferred characters in the course of one of the sections I had skipped.

From rereading to rereading, I made additional efforts to apprehend, to integrate into my vision of the whole, those pages I had at first skipped. But the decisive step was taken only when I received the long-awaited copy of *The Big Money.* Though I was at first disappointed not to find the names of any of the beloved characters of the first two volumes in the table of contents of this third, I was able, for the first time and without effort, to read the book from beginning to end, as the author would have wanted it to be read. (It is unquestionably a good thing that novelists, especially those whose technique is ambitious, are unaware of the bad habits of even their most impassioned and most conscientious readers.) For the first time, I not only did not skip, but felt from the beginning the *connections* between the stories as well as their novelistic continuity—perceiving immediately, for example, the subtle counterpoint formed by the newspaper headlines, the camera monologue, and the biographies of Ford, Hearst, and Valentino that surround the "solos" of Charley, Margo, and Mary French. Dos Passos's technique was finally proved efficacious.

An adaptation this complete to a technique so initially upsetting obviously presupposes a long familiarity with the work. But many writers would subscribe to Gide's declaration that he no longer writes except to be "reread" and would agree with him that they can only hope to win their case by "appeal." In addition, it can be said without paradox that the novel is the genre that most requires time in which to deliver up to us all its marrow, and that true comprehension of such a work begins only when the first superficial pleasure of reading, the elementary delight we all find in following a story, is over. The true reader of novels, the one every novelist worthy of the name should have, is not the man whose tastes are the most varied and whose culture is the most extensive but the one who tirelessly reads and rereads a small number of select works—Dickens, Meredith, or Balzac; *War and Peace, La Chartreuse de Parme,* or *À la Recherche du temps perdu.* One may advise such a reader, if he wishes from time to time to enrich his universe, to add to his list Bernanos, Graham Greene, or Dos Passos, even if the unraveling of these texts, the breaking into new territory, demands of him some small initial effort.

The reading of Dos Passos will compensate him not only by peopling the domains of his imagination with new creations but by refining and making more subtle his novelistic perception. His inner breadth, his receptivity to a certain literary polyphony, will be considerably augmented by the assimilation of a book like *The Big Money.* And though this quasi-gymnastic function of enlargement, of the modification of human awareness, is not the essential mission of art, it is not unimportant. The daring of first the impressionists and then the cubists gradually trained the public's eye, teaching it to apprehend immediately the beauty and meaning of pictures that fifty years earlier would have been considered unintelligible and scandalous chaos. The extent of man's plasticity is so undefined that there is almost an obligation for the writer to take advantage of the possibilities of the human spirit in order to transform systematically the novelistic vision of his contemporaries. (There is an analogous obligation for the painter, the filmmaker, the composer.) Joyce and Dos Passos, who were pioneers in this literary reeducation, understood this and thus predisposed readers to future works that will be even more subtle and complex than their own. More than for the specific contribution of their researches into the technique of the novel (for it is hard to see how a technique as personal and as closely adapted to the unique message of *U.S.A.* can be imitated), these authors deserve the thanks of future novelists for having prepared their public. Because of their efforts, the impersonal novel will perhaps some day be possible.

From this point of view, it is curious to note that the technique of Dos Passos's two later books, *Adventures of a Young Man* and *Number One,* marks, in relation to that of *The Big Money,* a sort of regression, a return to the traditional, individualistic form of the novel, centered on one character cut off from the elements that would integrate him with impersonal history. It is no less strange to note that the author of *Manhattan Transfer* underwent a gradual detachment from the novelistic genre. After he wrote *The Ground We Stand On* and a sociological study (remarkable, to be sure), *State of the Nation,* he wrote a life of Jefferson, a typically American hero. The reasons for this must be sought in the impasse to which a conception of the world such as his—one full of implicit contradictions, making for both the grandeur and the limitations of his work—must lead.

The specifically literary merits of Dos Passos are a perfect objectivity in the presentation of the facts, which he shares with many another American novelist of his generation, and a sort of untamed energy that he brings even to the portrayal of despair—an energy linked to a profound vitality that is also very American. What gives the best pages of *The Big Money* such an inimitable voice, what gives such value to the biographies of Hearst and Veblen, to the funeral oration of Sacco and Vanzetti, to the portrait of the vagabond that closes the book, is the union (which only Dos Passos was able to make work) of an extremely vehement tone with absolute impartiality. It is remarkable, for example, that nowhere in the biography of Hearst does he use his own voice to cast aspersions or to stigmatize; and yet we feel the vibration of his indignation, both passionate and contained, in every one of his sentences. This indictment by Dos Passos is not even primarily based on Hearst's specific or particular acts, but rather on his basic deficiency: more than the adversary of the League of Nations or the man responsible for Manila Bay, Hearst is the spoiled little boy who thinks himself Caesar and is not even Alcibiades, the man who never managed "to bridge the tiny Rubicon between amateur and professional politics," the man whose verdict will have to be the indifferent handful of earth thrown on his grave in the last two lines of his biography. Here lies "a spent Caesar grown old with spending—never man enough to cross the Rubicon."

Dos Passos can condemn, can *damn,* just by showing people as they are, by describing them faithfully, by drawing their outlines with an exactitude more implacable than could be achieved through any extravagance of tone. The note most indicative of his work, that which makes it unique, is this objective indignation. This is because his indignation goes beyond the individual to attack the whole system that has produced him—and not only, as orthodox Marxists are simple enough to believe, the capitalist system. Dos Passos's anger cannot help but be objective because it is directed ultimately against Being itself.

Thus, Samuel Insull, destroyed by the bankers and dragging the stockholders of his eighty-five companies into ruin with him, is by no means a vile scoundrel—or even a crooked financier or a dishonest director. He did nothing more than understand and exploit the truth formulated by Barnum in the celebrated phrase, "There's a sucker born every minute." Then he became the victim of the fragility of the capitalist system. He is not, as a man, hateful; he has only been the instrument of the order of things. The novelist does not have to judge his characters: he has neither the need nor the right to do so. The criticism of people and institutions will automatically take place in the mind of the reader, provided they are presented with truth and vigor. Dos Passos's art is the more convincing for its perfect objectivity.

But even this merit entails its opposite. If Dos Passos, conforming to the evangelical precept, thus abstains from any judgments, it is because he is fundamentally incapable of judging, for judgment presupposes an organized system of positive norms, of firm and cohesive certainties in whose name one can render a verdict. Dos Passos's message is as deliberately, as passionately, negative as Socrates's. Like Veblen, his favorite hero, he is congenitally incapable of an unambiguous "yes." It is quite clear, despite the apparent impartiality of his narration, that his political sympathies in *U.S.A.* go to all those who, like Eugene Debs and Thorstein Veblen, have been vanquished because they said "no!"—to dissidents of all types, to the Spanish anarchists, to the revolutionary Mexicans (among whom Mac, the only character in *U.S.A.* to find happiness, will go to live), to the members of the IWW, to those whose actions will probably never even get into the history books. His heroes are always heretics, like Glenn Spotswood or Ben Compton, excluded from the party for which they have sacrificed themselves, broken in body and spirit, having lost even the belief in the efficacy of their fight and their martyrdom, but keeping to the end that critical spirit affirmed by Glenn Spotswood's intellectual testament, written from the prison in which he was put by the Republicans: "I, Glenn Spotswood, being of sound mind and emprisoned body, do bequeath to the international working class my hope of a better world." It is significant that when Dos Passos (referring to the architect Frank Lloyd Wright) wants to make a list of the fundamental needs of man, he finds (like an Epicurean listing authentic pleasures) that only negative suggestions occur to him:

> (Tell us, doctors of philosophy, what are the needs of a man. At least a man needs to be notjailed notafraid nothungry notcold not without love, not a worker for a power he has never seen that cares nothing for the uses and needs of a man or a woman or a child.)[2]

It is easy to see why he does not express his anger in intellectual terms: he cannot. Indeed, it is hard to see in the name of what, by

---

[2] John Dos Passos, *1919*, Boston, Houghton Mifflin, 1946, p. 504.—Tr.

virtue of which doctrine, he *could* get angry. Veblen did not get angry either. At most, he allowed himself some occasional irony; in general, he merely set before his audience the contradictions of the system. Like him, throughout *U.S.A.* Dos Passos weaves the "logical inescapable rope of matter of fact for a society to hang itself by." He does not have to condemn his characters; they will destroy themselves on their own. There is nothing constructive, nothing positive, nothing affirmative, in his work, and in this way he escapes both the aridity of the thesis novel and the naïveté of the writer-saviors, who insist on propounding remedies against the incurable ill that is man's existence. He is all but forced to remain faithful to the great mission of literature, which is only to *show* reality, not to improve it.

At the same time, because of this profound negativism, his books will always seem somewhat lacking, almost incomplete. His protest goes much beyond political protest: he is quite obviously suspicious of all collectivities, all forms of society, of no matter what kind. Would Veblen really have been more at home in a communist regime? And Socrates? It is not a religious protest, either, given Dos Passos's deep-rooted and almost unconscious materialism (obvious, for example, in the enumeration of the fundamental human needs cited above); nor is it, given his extremely concrete nature, a metaphysical one, except implicitly. Ultimately, it is not easy to see clearly exactly what he is angry about; he is just angry, that is all. Very simply, he says *no*. If nothing were known of him but what comes through from his writing, it would be very easy to see the author of *The Big Money* as another Veblen—an old bear, stubborn and taciturn, that has ended up speaking only in growls:

> Veblen
> asked too many questions, suffered from a constitutional inability
> to say yes.
> Socrates asked questions, drank down the bitter drink one night
> when the first cock crowed,
> but Veblen
> drank it in little sips through a long life . . .[3]

[3] John Dos Passos, *The Big Money*, Boston, Houghton Mifflin, 1946, p. 107.—Tr.

But we know that Dos Passos, fortunately, did not drain the chalice to the dregs, at least not as Socrates or even Veblen did. What saves him from complete nihilism is undoubtedly his prodigious vitality, the extraordinary vigor that he cannot help but bring even to a message as passionately negative as his own. His denials are as positive, as energetic, as most people's affirmations. His books "end badly" in every conceivable way, and yet we are not depressed by reading them. At the end of *The Big Money* Charley Anderson is killed in a car accident; J. W. Moorehouse is growing old alone and embittered; Dick Savage, rotten at the core, like an overripe fruit, outlives himself, seeking a refuge in alcohol from the sense of the futility of his existence; Margo Dowling will certainly not be as great a star in sound films as she had been in the silents; and Eveline Hutchins commits suicide with an overdose of barbiturates.

The historical destinies are no more comforting: Isadora Duncan and Rudolph Valentino die tragically; Frank Lloyd Wright is the "patriarch of the new building/not without honor except in his own country"; Fred Taylor, the mystic of efficiency, dies in a fit of depression without having seen the fruition of his American Plan; Ford, stupidity itself, "the crackerbarrel philosopher," who has known only how to exploit the system until the moment when the system turns against him, grows old barricaded on the family farm, protected by an army of detectives and trembling with fear before the new America he has helped create, that of the strikers and the starving. Good or bad, egotistical or selfless, for capitalism—like Charley, Margo, and Tyler Spotswood—or against it—like Mary French, Glenn Spotswood, and Ben Compton—Dos Passos's characters are destined to failure, to death, or to an absurd martyrdom like Glenn's.

D. H. Lawrence, who loved the unflinching honesty of *Manhattan Transfer,* described it as "a great ravel of flights from nothing to nothing." This definition could quite accurately be applied to *U.S.A.*, which opens with a prologue entitled "Vag," in which we see a young man walking avidly among the nocturnal crowds of a big city, watching, listening, eager to grasp life with both hands—and which closes with an epilogue also entitled "Vag," in which a young man (and why not the same one?) is vainly waiting along the side of a highway, having realized none of his desires, having achieved nothing. For Dos Passos, the structure of the world in which we live is composed of what Jaspers calls the "cipher of failure," and it is this objective hieroglyph that he makes us see—like a watermark—on each page of his books.

Once these three volumes of *U.S.A.*, the apogee of failure and despair, were written—and with all desirable impartiality and rigor—it is not very clear what there remained for the author to do. In them he attained that point of perfection in the work of a writer where every merit becomes inseparable from a limitation. Since his two later novels do not in any sense constitute a renewal of his universe—not even an appreciable enrichment of it—I have in a sense spoken of them as if they were supplements to the trilogy that remains his masterpiece. The most curious thing about them is that they are a return to a narrative focused on an individual, which is rather astonishing on the part of a writer who had so deliberately set himself the task of creating an impersonal novel. But this is because Dos Passos (and Hemingway too, despite *For Whom the Bell Tolls*) always remained an impenitent individualist. As Orestes Brown noted, the reformation of the masses cannot be accomplished unless one first reforms the component individuals. In the final analysis, the only positive virtues Dos Passos puts any hope in are the strictly individual ones: he believes in a kind of artist's morality, difficult to make general, that consists of absolute honesty and rectitude of vision—the effort to arrive at the same implacable objectivity as the camera.

One can hardly suppose that Dos Passos was happy with his literary position. When Veblen's wife finally left him, he wrote to one of his friends: "The President doesn't approve of my domestic arrangements: nor do I." That "nor do I" is undoubtedly the only commentary that his position as artist will allow an aware and critical person like Dos Passos to make. His efforts to renew himself by means of sociological studies, biographies of Jefferson, etc., must be seen as the equivalent of the growls of a taciturn bear, which is how Veblen, at the end of his life, was reduced to communicating with his fellow men. When the novelistic idiom stutters, becomes disjointed, it is called reportage.

It is also difficult to believe that Dos Passos will manage to maintain his equilibrium, as he grows older, on the level of "happy-in-spite-of-all-despair" that he managed to reach in *U.S.A.*, even in its artistic expression. The "lion-become-old" will probably not be able to preserve the personal union, perhaps unique in literature, of the three antagonistic elements of nihilism, objectivity, and emotional violence. Judging from his latest works, it is not very likely that the unballasting will take place at the expense of impartiality and that he will cede to the temptation of a hopeless but vehement lyricism like that of Henry Miller, that American of Paris. It seems equally unlikely that his vision will acquire an optimism that could only be achieved at the expense of lucidity. What he most risks losing is the vital buoyancy (very "war-correspondent") that makes it possible to walk serenely between two abysses whose depths are quite clearly seen, and then to describe very objectively what has been measured. His work will thus perhaps continue to evolve in the direction of the "document"— impartial rather than gripping. With Dos Passos, the novel will have made itself so impersonal that it will no longer be fiction, a work of imagination perhaps capable (who knows?) of transforming the world.

The Radicalism of *U.S.A.*

by Walter B. Rideout

Sometimes in *U.S.A.* the producing class confronts the hired agents of the owning class, but the central opposition in these volumes is between "production" and "business," that division of function which is so basic to Veblen's thinking. Max Lerner has pointed out that the most clearly Veblenian character is Charley Anderson, the engineer who is trapped and broken by the power of business as though he were a "footnote" to *The Engineers and the Price System.* If one accepts the fact of Dos Passos's reliance on Veblen more than on Marx, it likewise becomes clear why there are no major characters from the owning class; they would simply be in the way of the author's intent. It is sufficient for his purpose that Charley Anderson's destruction should come when he attempts to shift from productive technician to unproductive tycoon, and that J. Ward Morehouse and the smaller parasite Dick Savage lose their integrity, create nothing of social value, and win the big money. As for the blankly beautiful Margo Dowling, the finest flower of this civilization, her apotheosis in the movie "industry" of Hollywood is a legend of conspicuous consumption, a living proof of the theory of the leisure class. Even Mary French, who sides with the class-conscious working class and would therefore be granted a fuller life by a Marxist writer, is affected by the social dry rot and doomed to sterile frustration.

Because of its dependence for ideological basis on Veblen's bitter drink, *U.S.A.* seems a somber and negative book; yet it contains a

"The Radicalism of *U.S.A.*" (editor's title). From Walter B. Rideout, *The Radical Novel in the United States: 1900–1954* (Cambridge, Mass.: Harvard University Press.), pp. 162–64. (Footnotes have been deleted.) Copyright, 1956, by the President and Fellows of Harvard College. Reprinted by permission of the publishers.

tentative affirmation. The positive hope of *U.S.A.* comes from Walt Whitman, of whose revolutionary quality Dos Passos wrote in answering the *Modern Quarterly* questionnaire. Even more than in *Manhattan Transfer* one sees that Whitman's love of the American spoken word lies behind Dos Passos's own colloquial style in the stories, and like the poet, the novelist has tried to include, not just New York, but all America in his work. Equally important, Dos Passos looks for the cure of his sick country, not to a dictatorship of the proletariat, but to a restoration—the word is significant—of the democratic vista. In Number 46 of the autobiographical Camera Eye sequences, the author presumably makes a soapbox speech in Union Square, trying to "talk straight" yet clutching quickly at the easy slogan:

> you suddenly falter ashamed flush red break out in sweat why not tell these men stamping in the wind that we stand on a quicksand? that doubt is the whetstone of understanding is too hard hurts instead of urging picket John D. Rockefeller the bastard if the cops knock your blocks off it's all for the advancement of the human race while I go home after a drink and a hot meal and read (with some difficulty in the Loeb Library trot) the epigrams of Martial and ponder the course of history and what leverage might pry the owners loose from power and bring back (I too Walt Whitman) our storybook democracy

Although a class struggle exists, the outcome envisaged by the author is not a new and historically determined synthesis, but rather the hoped-for overthrow of usurping owners and the *re*building of a democratic society. Thus the Sacco-Vanzetti Case stands as whatever climax the trilogy is allowed to have, and the next to the last two Camera Eye sequences shift to that brutal act on the part of America's owners in order to reveal the extent of their arrogance and their usurpation.

> how can I make them feel how our fathers our uncles haters of oppression came to this coast how say Don't let them scare you how make them feel who are your oppressors America
>   rebuild the ruined words worn slimy in the mouths of lawyers districtattorneys collegepresidents judges without the old words the im-

migrants haters of oppression brought to Plymouth how can you
know who are your betrayers America
or that this fishpeddler you have in Charlestown jail is one of your
founders Massachusetts?

To rebuild the words spoken at Plymouth and Paumanok, words
like "liberty" and "democracy," is for Dos Passos the answer, the
only answer, to the corrupt rulers of present-day America. If this
be Marx at all, it is surely Marx "Americanized."

After the publication of *The Big Money,* with its corrosive
sketches of a bureaucratized Party, the myth of "Comrade" Dos
Passos could not be maintained much longer. But back in 1930
young writers going Left found in him what they wanted, what
they needed to find—a real sympathy for "the oppressed and the
outcast" and a hard anger against the oppressors, both expressed
skillfully by a man accepted internationally as a major novelist. So
when they talked revolution in eager communion far into the
night or when they struggled to put into words their own new
vision of the U.S.A. or when, occasionally, on picket lines they sang
that song with its hymnlike refrain, "Which side are you on?," then
they could warm themselves with the happy, if inaccurate, conviction that Dos Passos too was with them all the way.

John Dos Passos: Technique vs. Sensibility

by Herbert Marshall McLuhan

Most elaborate of the many spoofs made by James Joyce was his obeisance to Dujardins as his "master" of the interior monolog. Only less elaborate have been the jokes played by Mr. Eliot, as in presenting to Harvard his copy of Jessie Weston with many pages uncut. To darken the counsel of those who choose to live in darkness has always been a form of light-bringing among the wits. But easily the most esoteric literary high-jinx of our time is the very formal debate, conducted far above the heads of Bloomsbury, between Wyndham Lewis and James Joyce. Lewis's "attack" on Joyce as a romantic time-snob, and Joyce's "counterattack" in *Finnegans Wake* are not just obscurantist trifling but a means of offering important insights of those readers who have acquired certain preliminary disciplines.

The reader of Dos Passos, however, is not required to have much more reading agility than the reader of the daily press. Nor does Dos Passos make many more serious demands than a good movie. And this is said not to belittle an excellent writer who has much to offer, but to draw attention to the extreme simplification to which Dos Passos has submitted the early work of James Joyce. *Three Soldiers* (1921), *Manhattan Transfer* (1925) and *U. S. A.* (1930–36) would not exist in their present form but for the *Portrait of the Artist as a Young Man*, *Dubliners* and *Ulysses*. It is as a slightly super-realist that Dos Passos has viewed and adapted the work of

"John Dos Passos: Technique vs. Sensibility" by Herbert Marshall McLuhan from *Fifty Years of the American Novel*, edited by Harold C. Gardiner, is reprinted by permission of Charles Scribner's Sons. Copyright 1951 Charles Scribner's Sons.

Joyce in his own work. And since his technical debt to Joyce is so considerable, one useful way of placing the achievement of Dos Passos is to notice what he took over and, especially, what he did not take.

As a young man in Chicago and at Harvard Dos Passos was much alive to the imagists, Sandburg, Fletcher, Pound, Amy Lowell and the French poet Cendrars. From them he learned much that has continuously affected his practice. Their romantic tapestries and static contemplation of the ornate panorama of existence have always held him in spite of his desire to be a romantic of action. The same conflict, between the man who needs to participate in the life of his time and the artist who wishes to render that life more luminous by self-effacement in his art, appears also in Whitman and in Hemingway. Hemingway's solution may prove to have been in some ways the most satisfactory insofar as he has succeeded occasionally in holding up the critical mirror to the impulse of romantic action, and not just to the action itself.

Dos Passos has been less sure than Hemingway of his artistic direction, though more confident in his politics. But everywhere from *One Man's Initiation* (1917) to the trilogy *U. S. A.* he has been conscious of the need for some sort of detachment and some sort of commitment. *Three Soldiers* is a portrait of the "artist" as G.I. in which, as in E. E. Cummings' *The Enormous Room,* the demand of the individual for some kind of intelligibility in a merely bureaucratic order is met by savage group-reprisal. That has remained the vision of Dos Passos.

For in recent decades the artist has come to be the only critical spectator of society. He demands and confers the heightened significance in ordinary existence which is hostile to any self-extinction in the collective consciousness. So that when the balance is lost between individual responsibility and mass solidarity, the artist automatically moves to the side of the individual. With equal inevitability, the less resourceful man, faced with the perplexities of planned social disorder, walks deeper into the collective sleep that makes that chaos bearable to him. The work of Dos Passos is almost wholly concerned with presenting this situation. His people are, typically, victims of a collective trance from which they do not struggle to escape. And if his work fails, it is to the extent that he clings to an alternative dream which has little power to retract the dreamers from their sleep, and even less power to alert the reader to a sense of tragic waste.

Born in 1896, John Dos Passos grew up in a milieu that had brought to a focus a number of discordant themes and motivations. The popularity of Darwin and Spencer had by then led to the profession of a doctrinaire individualism which got melodramatic treatment at the hands of a Frank Norris. Louis Sullivan and Frank Lloyd Wright were considerably affected by the spirit associated with the flamboyant extroversion and aggression of "frontier" Darwinism. Carl Sandburg's "Chicago" illustrates the curious blend of democratic lyricism and megalomaniac brutality that existed at that time. Robinson Jeffers has the gloomy distinction of representing today the then fashionable code of doctrinaire sadism which found a center in Chicago at the turn of the century.

Superficially it may appear odd that the cosmic humanitarianism of Whitman should have fostered such diverse expressions as the work of Sandburg and Jeffers. But as Sidney Lanier pointed out long ago, Whitman himself was a Byronic dandy turned inside out. Reared on the picturesque art of Scott with its preoccupation with the folk and their crafts, nurtured equally on the heroic panoramas of Byron with his vistas of world history, Whitman found no difficulty in transferring this aristocratic art to the democratic scene. Had not the aristocratic Chateaubriand earlier acquired in America the palette and the scenes which were to attract to him the discipleship first of Lord Byron and later of Stendhal and Flaubert? And the Jeffersonian dream of democracy was of a leveling-up rather than a leveling-down process. An aristocratic dream after all.

Co-existing with the fashionable Darwinism of mid-West tycoons was the grass-roots populism which found an academic spokesman in the formidable Thorstein Veblen. Veblen is ably presented in *The Big Money*, the last of the *U. S. A.* trilogy, as are Henry Ford and Sam Insull. Taken together, Veblen, Ford and Insull are strikingly representative of the unresolved attitudes and conflicts of the milieu in which Dos Passos grew up. Nor does Dos Passos attempt any reconciliation of these conflicts. While his sympathies are entirely with the agrarian Veblen and the grass-roots, his art is committed to rendering the entire scene. And it is attention to the art of Dos Passos that the critic finds most rewarding. For Dos Passos is not a thinker who has imposed a conceptual system on his material. Rather, he accepted the most familiar traditions and attitudes as part of the material which his art brings into the range of the reader's vision. It is by the range of his vision and the intensity of his focus that he must receive criticism.

As a boy in Chicago, Dos Passos was devoted to Gibbon's *Decline and Fall of the Roman Empire*. Artistically, Gibbon's late use of baroque perspectivism, the linear handling of history as a dwindling avenue, concurred with the eighteenth-century discovery of the picturesque, or the principle of discontinuity as a means of enriching artistic effect. So that the later discovery of contemporary imagism and impressionism by Dos Passos, and his enthusiasm for the cinematic velocity of images in the French poet Cendrars, corresponded pretty much with the original revolution in eighteenth-century taste and perception which carried letters from the style of Gibbon to Sterne.

Looking first at the technical means which he employs as a writer, there is the basic imagistic skill in sharpening perception and defining a state of mind with which *Manhattan Transfer* opens:

> Three gulls wheel above the broken boxes, orangerinds, spoiled cab-
> bage heads that heave between the splintered plank walls, the green
> waves spume under the round bow as the ferry, skidding on the tide,
> crashes, gulps the broken water, slides, settles slowly into the slip.

Many passages of this wry lyricism counterpoint the episodes of the book. The episodes and characters are also features of a landscape to which these lyric chapter overtures give point and tone. The point is readily seized and the tone extends over a very narrow range of emotions: pathos, anger, disgust. But Dos Passos employs the impressionist landscape monotonously because he has never chosen to refract or analyze its components to zone a wide range of emotions. Open any page of Pound's *Cantos* and the same impressionist landscapes will be found to be presenting a variety of carefully-discriminated mental states. Pound does not accept the landscape as a homogeneous lump of matter. Even satire is managed by Dos Passos in a direct, lyric mode though the technique seems to be impersonal:

> He's darn clever and has a lot of personality and all that sort of thing, but all he does is drink and raise Cain . . . I guess all he needs is to go to work and get a sense of values.

or:

> The terrible thing about having New York go stale on you is that there's nowhere else. It's the top of the world. All we can do is go round and round in a squirrel cage.

Manhattan Transfer is full of such planned incongruities which achieve a weak pathos when they could more successfully have effected a robust guffaw. The author is sensitive to the ugliness and misery as things he can see. But he is never prepared to explore the interior landscape which is the wasteland of the human heart:

> Ellen stayed a long time looking in the mirror, dabbing a little superfluous powder off her face, trying to make up her mind. She kept winding up a hypothetical dollself and setting it in various positions. Tiny gestures ensued, acted out on various model stages. Suddenly she turned away . . . "Oh, George I'm starved, simply starved . . . we've got to be sensible. God knows we've messed things up in the past both of us . . . Let's drink to the crime wave."

The effect is comparable to that of *That Great Gatsby,* which sustains this Hansel and Gretel sort of wistful despair to creat a child-pastoral world. Out of the same situations Hemingway at his best—as in the first page of *A Farewell to Arms*—can obtain moments of tragic intensity—landscapes of muted terror which give dignity to human suffering.

But Dos Passos too often seems to imply that the suffering is sordid and unnecessary or that some modification of the environment might free his characters from the doll-mechanism that is their private and collective trap. Seeing nothing inevitable or meaningful in human suffering, he confronts it neither in its comic, intelligible mode, nor in a tragic way. It angers and annoys him as something extraneous.

The difference from Joyce is instructive. For in *Ulysses* the same discontinuous city landscape is also presented by imagistic devices. The episodes are musically arranged to sound concordantly. But Joyce manipulates a continuous parallel at each moment between naturalism and symbolism to render a total spectrum of outer and inner worlds. The past is present not in order to debunk Dublin but to make Dublin representative of the human condition. The sharply-focussed moment of natural perception in Joyce floods the situation with analogical awareness of the actual dimensions of human hope and despair. In *Ulysses* a brief glimpse of a lapidary at work serves to open up ageless mysteries in the relations of men and in the mysterious qualities of voiceless objects. The most ordinary gesture linked to some immemorial dramatic mask or situation sets reverberating the whole world of the book and flashes intelligibility into long opaque areas of our own experience.

To match Joyce's epiphanies Dos Passos brings only American know-how. And, indeed, there seems to be no corner of the continent with whose speech and cooking he is not familiar. There is no trade or profession which he does not seem to know from the inside. Joyce contemplates things for the being that is theirs. Dos Passos shows how they work or behave.

Earlier, Joyce had opened the *Portrait* with an overture representative of the stages of human apprehension, which with Aristotle he held to be a shadow of the artistic process itself, so that the development of the artist concurs with the retracing of the process of poetic experience. By a technique of cubist or overlayering perspectives both of these processes are rendered present to the reader in an instant of inclusive consciousness. Hence the "portrait" claim of the title. The very setting side-by-side of these two operations is typical, therefore, of the level and extent of symbolic implication in Joyce. (The Oxen of the Sun section of *Ulysses* fused both these processes with both the human biological and civilized processes, as well as with the parts and totality of the book itself, and yet has been read as a series of parodies of English prose styles.)

The difference between this kind of art and that of Dos Passos is that between one of univocal, psychological and one of properly analogical effect. Joyce constantly has his attention on the analogy of being while Dos Passos is registering a personal reaction to society.

It is not a serious criticism of Dos Passos to say that he is not James Joyce. But Joyce is his art master and the critic is obliged to note that Dos Passos has read Joyce not as a greater Flaubert, Rimbaud or Mallarmé, but as it were through the eyes of Whitman and Sandburg, as a greater Zola or Romains. This is negative definition which does not bring into question the competence of Dos Passos or belittle the quality of positive delight he affords. His *U. S. A.* is quite justly established as a classic which brought into a focus for the first time a range of facts and interests that no American had ever been able to master. But it is in the main an ethical and political synthesis that he provides, with the interest intentionally at one level—the only level that interests Dos Passos.

Manhattan Transfer, which corresponds roughly to Joyce's *Dubliners,* cuts a cross-section through a set of adult lives in New York. But the city is not envisaged as providing anything more than a phantasmagoric back-drop for their frustrations and defeats. The city is felt as alien, meaningless. Joyce, on the other hand, accepts the city as an extension of human functions, as having a human shape and eliciting the full range of human response which man cannot achieve in any other situation. Within this analogy Joyce's individuals explore their experience in the modes of action and passion, male and female. The stories are grouped according to the expanding awareness of childhood, adolescence, maturity and middle-age. Man, the wanderer within the labyrinthine ways at once of his psyche and of the world, provides an inexhaustible matter for contemplation. Dos Passos seems to have missed this aspect of *Dubliners.* But in *U. S. A.,* while extending his back-drop from the city to the nation, he did make the attempt to relate the expanding scene to the development of one mind from childhood to maturity. That is the function of "Camera Eye." "News-reel" projects the changing environment which acts upon the various characters and corresponds to riffling the back issues of *Life* magazine.

But *Ulysses,* with which *U. S. A.* invites comparison, shows a very different conception of history in providing a continuous parallel between ancient and modern. The tensions set up in this way permit Joyce to control the huge accretions of historic power and suggestion in the human past by means of the low-current of immediate incident. The technological analog of this process occurs in the present use of the electronic valve in heavy-power circuits. So that Joyce does not have to step up the intensity of the episode or scene so long as he maintains its function in the total circuit. Deprived of this symbolic "feed-back" process implicit in the historic sense, and which is manipulated alike by Joyce, Pound and Eliot, Dos Passos is left with little more current or intensity than that generated by his immediate episodes.

Since criticism, if it is to be anything more than a review of the "content" of works of art, must take cognizance of the technical means by which an artist achieves his effects, it is relevant to consider some of the stages by which the kind of art found in *U. S. A.* came into existence. If there is anything to be explained about such a work it can best be done by noting the extraordinary preoccupation with landscape in eighteenth-century art. For it was the discovery of the artistic possibilities of discontinuity that gave their form to the novels of Scott as well as to the poems of Byron and Whitman.

Whitman, a great reader of Scott in his youth, later took pains to bring into his poetry as much of the contemporary technology as he could manage. Whitman's poems are also camera-eye landscapes in which human tasks are prominent. In his numerous portraits which he strove to bring into line with the techniques of the impressionists' painting, he wove the man's work into his posture and gestures. His aim was to present the actual, and he took pride that in his *Leaves of Grass* "everything is literally photographed." As for the larger lines of his work, it is plain that he uses everywhere a cinematic montage of "still" shots.

It is not only in the details but in the spirit of much of his work that Whitman resembles Dos Passos. And it is hard to see how anyone who set himself to rendering the diverse existence of multitudes of people could dispense with the technique of discontinuous landscapes. In fact, until the technique of discontinuous juxtaposition was brought into play it was not even possible to entertain such an ambition. "Remember," he said of the *Leaves* to Dr. Bucke, "the book arose out of my life in Brooklyn and New York from 1838 to 1853, absorbing a million people, for fifteen years, with an intimacy, an eagerness, an abandon, probably never equalled." Taken in connection with his technical inventiveness, this enables us to see why the French were from the start so much more interested in Whitman than either his countrymen or the English. Hopkins, struggling with similar technical problems at a more serious level, remarked, however, that he had more in common with Whitman than with anybody else of his time.

From this point of view it is plain, also, why Tolstoy and Hugo could take Scott and Byron with the same artistic seriousness with which Dostoevsky regarded Dickens. Dickens was probably the first to apply the picturesque to discoveries in technique, to the entire life of an industrial metropolis. And the brilliance of his technical development of this matter provided W. D. Griffiths with his cinematic principles seventy years later.

However, it was in Flaubert's *Sentimental Education* that the acceptance of the city as the central myth or creation of man first leads to the mastery of that huge material by means of the technique of discontinuous landscape. Moreover, Flaubert makes a continuous parallel between the fatuity of Frederic Moreau's "education" and the deepening sordor and banality of nineteenth-century Paris.

It is slightly otherwise in *U. S. A.*, where the development of political consciousness of the "Camera Eye" persona is not so much parallel with as in contrast to the unfolding landscape of the nation. And this again is close to the way in which the development of Stephen Dedalus in the *Portrait* as a self-dedicated human being runs counter to the mechanisms of the Dublin scene. The author's political and social sense unfolds without comment in the "Camera

Eye" sections, with "News-reel" providing the immediate environmental pressures which are felt in different ways by everybody in the book. Both of these devices are successfully controlled to provide those limited effects which he intends. But the insights which lead to these effects are of a familiar and widely accepted kind.

That, again, in no way invalidates the insights but it does explain the monotony and obviousness which creeps into so many pages. The reader of Dos Passos meets with excellent observation but none of the unending suggestiveness and discovery of the *Sentimental Education* or *Ulysses*. For there is neither historical nor analogical perception in the *U. S. A.*, and so it fails to effect any connections with the rest of human society, past or present. There is a continuous stream of American consciousness and an awareness that there are un-American elements in the world. But as much as in any political orator there is the assumption that iniquity inside or outside the U. S. A. is always a failure to be true to the Jeffersonian dream. The point here is that this kind of single-level awareness is not possible to anybody seriously manipulating the multiple keyboards of Joyce's art.

Dickens as a newspaper reporter had hit upon many of his characteristic effects in the course of his daily work. Later, when he turned to the serial publication of his stories, he was compelled to do some of that "writing backwards" which, as Edgar Poe saw, is the principle underlying the detective story and the symbolist poem alike. For in both instances the effect to be attained is the point at which the writer begins. The work finally constructed is a formula for the effect which is both the beginning and the end of the work.

It is interesting to note how Browning moved toward a fusion of these interests in the *Ring and the Book*, turning a police romance into a cross-section of an inclusive human consciousness by the technique of the reconstruction of a crime. Artistically he is more complex than Dos Passos in the use he makes of the dramatic process of retracing or reconstruction. For that retracing reveals many of the labyrinthine recesses of the human heart which the merely panoramic impressionism of Dos Passos cannot even attempt to do. And it is also this profound drama of retracing the stages of an experience which enables the popular detective story to sound varied depths of the greatest human themes in the hands of Graham Greene. In the art of Eliot (as in *The Cocktail Party*) it permits the sleuth and the guardian of souls to meet in the figure of Harcourt-Reilly, as in Browning's Pope.

The failure of Dos Passos' insights to keep pace with the complex techniques at his disposal is what leaves the reader with the sense of looseness and excessive bulk in *U. S. A.* In the equally bulky *Finnegans Wake,* on the other hand, which exploits all the existing techniques of vision and presentation in a consummate orchestration of the arts and sciences, there is not one slack phrase or scene. *U. S. A.,* by comparison, is like a Stephen Foster medley played with one finger on a five keyboard instrument. There is that sort of discrepancy between the equipment and the ensuing concert; but it is not likely to disturb those readers who have only a slight acquaintance with Joyce.

Manhattan Transfer and the *U. S. A.* trilogy are not novels in the usual sense of a selection of characters who influence and define one another by interaction. The novel in that sense was a by-product of biological science and as such persists today only among book-club practitioners. The novel as it has been concerned with the problems of "character" and environment seems to have emerged as a pastime of the new middle classes who were eager to see themselves and their problems in action. Remove from these novels the problems of money and the arts of social distinction and climbing and little remains. From that point of view Flaubert's *Madame Bovary* was the deliberate reduction of the middle-class novel to absurdity. And Sinclair Lewis's *Babbitt* is, as Ford Madox Ford pointed out, the American *Madame Bovary*. But the *Sentimental Education* is a great step beyond this, and taken with *Bouvard and Pecuchet,* provided the framework for the symbolic epic of the commonplace which is *Ulysses*. The middle classes found romance and glamour in the commonplace, but they were not prepared for the profound existentialist metaphysic of the commonplace which Joyce revealed.

In such a perspective as this the collective landscapes of *U. S. A.* represent only a modest effort at managing the huge panorama of triviality and frustration which is the urban milieu of industrial man.

But the fact that a technological environment not only induces most people into various stages of automatism but makes the family unit socially non-effective, has certainly got something to do with the collective landscapes of *U. S. A.* Its structure is poetic in having its unity not in an idea but a vision; and it is cubist in presenting multiple simultaneous perspectives like a cycle of medieval mystery plays. It could readily be maintained that this method not only permits comprehensiveness of a kind indispensable to the modern artist, but makes for the intelligible rather than the concupiscible in art. The kind of pleasure that Dos Passos provides in comparison with Hemingway is that of detached intellectual intuition rather than that of sympathetic merging with the narrative and characters.

The current conception of art as vicarious experience, on the other hand, seems mainly to support the attitude of behavioristic merging with the lives of the characters portrayed. And since this tendency is geared commercially with the demands of an untrained reader mass, it is irresistible. It helps to explain why a Dos Passos is considered high-brow although he offers no more strain on the attention than a detective story. It is because of the kind rather than the degree of effort he invites that he is deprecated as high-brow by readers who accept the cubist landscapes of the newspaper, and the musical equivalent in jazz, without perturbation.

Although Dos Passos may be held to have failed to provide any adequate intellectual insight or emotion for the vast landscape of his trilogy, his themes and attitudes are always interesting, especially in the numerous biographies of such folk heroes as Edison and the Wright brothers, Debs and La Follette, Steinmetz and Isadora Duncan, Ford and Burbank. These sections are often masterly in their economy and point. The frustration of hopes and intentions in these public figures provides the main clue to the social criticism which underlies the presentation of dozens of nonentities. For it is usually pointed up that the great are as helplessly ensnared in merely behavioristic patterns irrelevant to their own welfare, as the crowd of nobodies who admire them.

The frustration and distortion of life common to the celebrated and the obscure is, in Dos Passos, to be attributed to "the system." No diagnosis as crude as this emerges directly. But over and over again in the contrast between humble humanity and the gormandizing power-gluttony of the stupidly arrogant few, there is implied the preference for a world of simple, unpretentious folk united in their common tasks and experience. It has often been noted that there is never love between the characters of Dos Passos. But there is the pathos of those made incapable of love by their too successful adjustment to a loveless system. Genuine pathos is the predominant and persistent note in Dos Passos, and must be considered as his personal response to the total landscape. Yet it is a pathos free from self-pity because he has objectified it in his analysis of the political and economic situation.

The homelessness of his people is, along with their individual and collective incapacity for self-criticism or detachment, the most obvious feature about them. And home is the positive though unstated and undefined dream of Dos Passos. In wandering from the Jeffersonian ideal of a farmer-craftsman economy in the direction of Hamiltonian centralism, power and bigness, Dos Passos sees the main plight of his world. Hamilton set up the false beacon that brought shipwreck. But out of that shipwreck, which he depicts, for example, as the success of Henry Ford's enterprise, we can recover the dream and create a reality worthy of it. That is an unfailing note. For those who are critically aware he prescribes the duty of selfless dedication to the improvement of the common civilization. And in three uninteresting, short novels since *U. S. A.* he has explored the problem of discovering a self worth giving to such a cause. The current need would seem to be for a historic sense which can resolve the Hamilton-Jefferson dichotomy.

There is, perhaps, little point in dwelling on these aspects of Dos Passos, in which without new insight he reflects the ordinary attitude of the great majority. Yet, there is great social hope in the fact that this common intellectual ground is so large and so admirably chosen. But it is outside the province of criticism, which is concerned with the means employed and effects obtained by an artist. By the time the critic comes to the point of confronting Dos Passos the Jeffersonian radical, he has moved into a territory shared by Frank Capra.

And Dos Passos may have lost his stride as an artist through the very success of those social causes which were the militant theme of *U. S. A.* To have a cause to defend against a blind or indifferent world seemed to give tone and snap to the artist in him who has since been overlaid by the reporter. But if this is the case, nobody would be happier than Dos Passos to have lost his artistry on such excellent terms.

The Gullivers of Dos Passos

by Arthur Mizener

During the Forties and the Fifties John Dos Passos has very nearly achieved the rank of a neglected novelist. In the Twenties with the publication of *Three Soldiers* (1921) and *Manhattan Transfer* (1925) he was one of the promising young novelists, *Three Soldiers* particularly striking its period as a daring and realistic novel. In the Thirties the three novels that constitute *U.S.A.* gave him the reputation of having written "the American collective novel" at a time when everyone took the collective novel pretty seriously. These reputations were all misleading.

Three Soldiers is mainly an "art novel," the story of a young man too sensitive and esthetically aware to endure the crude world, who is defeated by that world; it is only incidentally the exposé of the Army in the First World War, which gave it its initial reputation with a decade very much concerned to come to terms with the war. *U.S.A.* is something different—and better—than the collective novel in which, as the fashion of the Thirties required, "the real hero . . . is society itself." The real hero of the book is a state of mind, a moral attitude toward our society and, by clear implication, all social organization. And a very "uncollective" state of mind it is, too ("when you try to find the people, always in the end it comes down to somebody").

Probably the Thirties' decision that *U.S.A.* was a collective novel was as unavoidable as the former decision that *Three Soldiers* was a realistic novel about the war. The form of the collective novel had been adumbrated by fashionable critics and proved in theory to be the one demanded by the times. They were nearly as certain to turn up a collective novel as was the eighteenth century to turn up a noble savage; and Dos Passos has suffered about as much from his selection for the first honor as Omai did from his selection for the second.

As Dos Passos has gone on producing the kind of novel he started to develop with *Manhattan Transfer,* his work has been less and less well received. The professional Left found *Adventures of a Young Man* (1938) grossly offensive; here, believe it or not, was the collective novelist himself passionately damning the conduct of the Communist Party in the Spanish Civil War and generally conducting himself like a Trotskyite. *Number One* (1943) was deplored as a journalistic novel about Huey Long. *The Grand Design* (1949) seemed painfully unenlightened to the numerous and influential liberals who had gone into the New Deal; think of Dos Passos setting up a prosperous businessman, almost a "malefactor of great wealth," as his hero and then having him defeated by the confusion, the egotism, and the selfishness of New-Deal liberals! This was unkind; this was betrayal. It has been a final misfortune for Dos Passos during these years that his kind of novel must carefully avoid the minute shading of character and the sensitive poetical style which have been the main current fashions in the novel, so that even the people who ought to have been reading and admiring him quietly while the liberals disowned him have (with a few honorable exceptions like Alfred Kazin) neglected him.

It was apparently useless to protest these irrelevant but damaging judgments during the Thirties and Forties; when T. K. Whipple remarked of *U.S.A.* in 1938 that in it "the class struggle is presented as a minor theme; the major theme is the vitiation and degradation of character in such a civilization," nobody minded him.[1] But enough time has passed now so that we ought to be able to see —instead of debating whether he takes a political position we happen at the moment to agree with or whether he writes in a style

1. [For T. K. Whipple's article see pp. 87–92 of this volume.—Ed.]

more or less like Virginia Woolf's—what Dos Passos has been doing. To look at him thus seeingly is, I believe, to discover that Dos Passos is a good novelist of a kind almost unique in our time.

What we need to recognize above all is the kind of novel Dos Passos is writing, the genre to which his work belongs. The best way to do that is to approach it by way of the tradition of comedy exemplified in slightly different ways by Ben Jonson and Swift. Dos Passos is not, I assume, consciously working in a literary tradition; neither was Swift. And Jonson is a great writer not because he had read and borrowed from the classics but because of the intensity of his vision of human experience. "He invades [classical] authors like a monarch," as Dryden put it; "and what would be theft in other poets is only victory in him." Yet Jonson, like Dos Passos, has suffered from the charge that—in his case because of slavish imitation of the classics—he is full of typed characters without the charm and warmth that romantically inclined people think is the whole value of Shakespeare's characters (and never know what to do with Timon and Coriolanus). Jonson, we are told, did not allow his characters to come alive and be human because he was too anxious to manipulate them like puppets in order to prove some commonplace moral fetched from the classics.

It is true, of course, that Jonson's characters are two-dimensional, calculatedly and necessarily, and that the moral values of his plays are, in one sense, familiar. Yet, for all their familiarity, they have hardly impressed themselves on us deeply enough to make humanity live by them. Doctor Johnson, speaking of another kind of romantic taste, made the best defense of Jonson's kind of poetry. "Those writers who lay on the watch for novelty," he said, "could have little hope of greatness; for great things cannot have escaped former observation." What matters finally in any kind of literature is not the novelty of its attitudes and values or the superficial charm and colorfulness of its characters but the realized and communicated passion for "the great things."

If a writer sees people, as writers like Jonson and Dos Passos do, not as aggregations of charming eccentricities, as "characters," but as representative cases, each of whom contributes in his way to our understanding of the drift of the community's life, and if he sees them thus with passion and intelligence, then he will produce neither romance nor tragedy but the most serious kind of satiric comedy, works like *Bartholomew Fair* or *Le Misanthrope* or *Gulliver's Travels* or *Adventures of a Young Man.* Such a work is immediately ironic about the shortcomings of its own society and, beyond that, about the permanent defects of humanity; it will seem to writers like these the most serious kind of work they can produce. "For if men will impartially, and not asquint, look toward the offices and functions of a poet," as Ben Jonson put it about his own work, "they will easily conclude to themselves the impossibility of any man's being a good poet, without first being a good man . . . it being the office of a comic poet to imitate justice, and instruct to live. . . ."

Therefore Jonson, basing his attack on the humanistic and Christian attitude professed by his age, held up to deadly ridicule the capitalist acquisitiveness and puritan pretentiousness of the early seventeenth century. Therefore Swift, basing his attack on the Christian reason and the benevolence professed by the eighteenth century, attacked (at least on the whole; he is a more complicated case than Jonson) the functionless ritual and the brutality of his society. With both writers the ultimate object of attack was man himself, that "most pernicious race of little odious vermin," as the King of Brobdingnag put it, "that nature ever suffered to crawl upon the surface of the earth." In the same way Dos Passos, taking quite seriously the anarchistic individualism and the egalitarianism of the American democratic tradition, attacks with satire the institutionalized corruption and the disintegrated private lives produced by the two mighty opposites of our society—industry and politics.

The characteristic novel form for comedy of this kind is the picaresque tale which carries its hero through a series of socially representative adventures (*The Adventures* of—Joseph Andrews, Roderick Random, A Young Man—is the formula for the title of the picaresque novel). This hero may be a young man of innocent and incurable good will, like the early Gulliver; or he may be the equally innocent rascal who believes that happiness is to be obtained by being smart and financially successful, like Volpone (except that after almost two centuries of benevolence Dos Passos's Volpones and Jonathan Wilds tend to be pathetic as well as vicious). In either case he is finally destroyed or at least defeated, if possible by the most pretentiously righteous institution of his society.

As in all fiction of this kind, there is in Dos Passos's work a lively, almost journalistic interest in the manners and customs of the Several Remote Nations into which his Gullivers travel. Just as Ben Jonson never overlooked a chance to work into his comedies a "humorous" portrait of an Elizabethan rascal or fool, so Dos Passos's work is full of comic portraits of American types, of bootleggers and Vassar girls, hillbillies and bankers, movie stars and labor bosses, radio pundits and merchant seamen; it would be difficult to name a type in our society which does not appear in Dos Passos. But always, from the day Fainy McCreary had to decide between his feelings for Maisie and his loyalty to the IWW, the core of Dos Passos's work has been an isolating, individual struggle between stubborn idealism and the corrupting forces of an organized society which demands conformity.

The passion of Swift's work comes to its sharpest focus in his hatred of the organized selfishness and hypocrisy of society: "I have ever hated all nations, professions, and communities, and all my love is toward individuals. . . . Principally I hate and detest that animal called man, although I heartily love John, Peter, Thomas, and so forth. . . ." The passion of Dos Passos's work is of exactly this kind. People may suppress the John, Peter, Thomas in themselves, as does Dick Savage when he sacrifices Daughter to conformity and success; but they die inside. Or they may insist on preserving it at any cost, as does Glenn Spotswood. In Dos Passos this cost is always not less than everything; these people are always destroyed by organized society, by the organized middle class, by organized business or labor or politics (standard American, which destroyed Tyler Spotswood, or CP, which destroyed Glenn).

Dos Passos was some time in arriving at the picaresque form which would allow full play to all these feelings, but he began to work toward it in *Manhattan Transfer*. In the book's wonderful panorama of representative American lives, of manners and customs, the lives of Ellen Thatcher and Jimmy Herf stand out. The last we see of Ellen she is on her way to meet George Baldwin, for whom she is divorcing Jimmy. "There are lives to be lived," she thinks, "if only you didn't care. Care for what, for what; the opinion of mankind, money, success, hotel lobbies, health, umbrellas, Uneeda biscuits. . . ? As she goes through the shining soundless revolving door . . . there shoots through her a sudden pang of something forgotten. . . . What did I forget in the taxicab?" What she forgot was her life. But the last we see of Jimmy Herf he is pulling out, down to his last three cents and hitching a ride with a redheaded truck driver. " 'How fur ye going?' 'I dunno. . . . Pretty far.' "

Through *The 42nd Parallel* and *Nineteen Nineteen* the magnificent panorama of American lives continues. In construction, in the controlled and integrated organization of an immense variety of characters Dos Passos goes way beyond Swift. This is structure as Jonson understood it in *The Alchemist,* the kind of organization Coleridge was thinking of when he said *The Alchemist* had one of the three perfect plots in the world. But it is only, I believe, with *The Big Money* that Dos Passos achieves the fully developed form of his kind of fiction. In *The Big Money* the attitude of tragic satire, the unwavering sense of the hero's essential innocence, the grim humor of his defeat dominate the novel; and there emerges the full picaresque form in which the hero's life is central and the ironic account of the manners of his world, however detailed, becomes the circumstances of his destruction. As Malcolm Cowley remarked of the book when it was first published, "We are likely to remember it as a furious and somber poem written in a mood of revulsion even more powerful than that which T. S. Eliot expressed in *The Waste Land.*" The effect of *U.S.A.* as a whole is the effect of a world in which no one wins, whether he "succeeds," as do Richard Savage and Margo Dowling and Charley Anderson, or fails, as do Mary French and Ben Compton and Eveline Hutchins. Their defeat in either case is a defeat beyond social or political redress, perhaps beyond human redress of any kind.

Since *The Big Money* Dos Passos has continued to write satiric comedies like it. The Gullivers change from novel to novel. Count-

ing both Charley Anderson and Tyler Spotswood there are two
innocent—and therefore finally pathetic—rascals who, like Ellen
Thatcher, discover too late that they have left something in the
taxicab ("I want to talk like we used to when, you know, up the Red
River fishin' when there wasn't any," says the dying Charley Anderson). And there are two stubbornly innocent idealists.

In *Adventures of a Young Man,* Glenn Spotswood really believes
in the ideals of Communism and is therefore excommunicated and
eventually murdered by the Party. In *Grand Design* Millard Carroll
believes in the same way in the ideals of the New Deal and is thrown
into the discard along with it when the war comes along. The stubborn esthetic resistance to the world of John Andrews in *Three Soldiers* has gradually changed through the course of Dos Passos's work
to the stubborn unworldliness of the Good American. Each of these
heroes is the predestined victim of all the forces of compromise and
corruption in his immediate society. Like the comic victims of all
works of this kind—like Don Quixote and Alceste and Candide, like
Sir Fopling Flutter and Joseph Andrews and Gulliver—the hero
allows his author to show how greed and lust in their various local
American forms operate to destroy the virtues American society is
supposed to live by. Each has the innocence and the incurable purity
of motive of the genuine idealist ("Tyler, what I'd started to write
you about was not letting them sell out too much of the for the
people and by the people part of the old-time United States way").
Each has, too, the primness, for Dos Passos can, like all good comic
writers, see that his hero's stubborn goodness is not only touching
but in the circumstances grimly funny.

Around each of these heroes Dos Passos constructs his wonderfully
varied, satiric representation of a segment of American society, of
the business world, of the labor movement, of professional politics,
of New-Deal Washington. Each subordinate character fits his part
in the whole by being what Jonson would have called a "humor."
You cannot easily forget Marice Gulick or Comrade Irving Silver-
stone or Chuck Crawford or Herbert Spotswood; you remember
them not because they seem "real" to you but because, like Sir Epi-
cure Mammon, they are classic representations of their types,

warmed to the kind of life all great satirists can create by the anger and grief of their author at finding them what they are. "Who but must laugh, if such a man there be? / Who would not weep, if Atticus were he?"

All these characters are held together by the beautifully integrated action. From the point of view of strict verisimilitude Dos Passos's story has far too many coincidences, just as it has far too many type characters. Glenn Spotswood, for instance, meets the Gulicks when he is a student and even lives in their house for a while; Tyler meets them when he is working for Chuck Crawford; Millard Carroll begins his career in Washington by having dinner with them. If your standards are those of the realistic novel you will be annoyed to find that every liberal academic economist no matter where he turns up is always Mike Gulick. But you might as well protest against Swift that of all the possible men in boats it is always Lemuel Gulliver who gets stranded on odd islands. Each of Dos Passos's minor characters leads a representative life; that life is related to other representative lives in typical ways. If we are to see Dos Passos's world whole, we must see how each of these lives impinges on every other one. In a fiction where the characters are typical, such coincidents— as long as they are individually plausible—are truer than random events would be. Dos Passos's greatest imaginative achievement is to have constructed this complex, minutely detailed, and yet tightly interlocked pattern of lives; it is the equivalent in his work of Faulkner's genealogy.

Just as the pattern of the story is designed to emphasize the representative nature of the characters, so is Dos Passos's style. Except for the Camera Eye in *U.S.A.* and the interspersed prose poems of direct moralizing in the later novels, which seem to me a mistake, he writes in a flat, deadly accurate, and devastating prose which reduces events and motives to what seems to Dos Passos their essential horror. These qualities are particularly evident in the last three novels, from the moment when Glenn defies the concentratedly fatuous Dr. Talcott at Camp Winnesquam to the final scene between Paul Graves and Walker Watson. They are most brilliantly demonstrated in the dialogue, in Joe Yerkes's wonderfully banal CP jargon, in Marice's fashionable drawing-room Freudian chatter, in Chuck Crawford's quintessential demagoguery, in Jerry Evans's bullying businessman's jocularity. Dos Passos's characters do not speak the language of the unique and special, the "interesting" personality; they speak with the voices of whole kinds, concentrated to cliché and glowing with Dos Passos's sad scorn for their terrible inadequacy. His novels are a nightmare of people damned to go on muttering forever "our beautiful lake . . . our lifegiving air," "wanted to observe complexes in various social stratifications," "hadn't been able to restrain her bourgeois possessive feelings," "this great worldwide effort to block the advance of tyranny and barbarism," "the case of those poor damned oil men."

To say that the talk and the feelings of Dos Passos's people are commonplace is to miss altogether the governing irony of his work: one might as well say that Polonius or The Citizen in "Ulysses" are not always so intelligent or original as they might be. To say that Dos Passos's judgment of our world is the application to it of perfectly familiar values is to ignore what makes his work the imposing indictment it is, that is, the passionate sincerity of his hatred of our failure, of humanity's failure, to be what it professes—and what it ought—to be.

The Chronicles of Dos Passos

by Richard Chase

The longer John Dos Passos writes, the more one admires his integrity, his hard-won skill, his capacity for work, and whether one agrees with him or not, the forthrightness of his political views. He looks good, too, in relation to the general run of new novelists; compared with their thin volumes of personal analysis, there is something grand about Dos Passos' massively researched and solidly constructed social novels. Yet the fact remains that in the last two decades Dos Passos' reputation has not fared so well as those of other writers of his generation—Faulkner, Hemingway, F. Scott Fitzgerald —nor does time seem likely to redress the balance.

In recent years Dos Passos has directed a good deal of cantankerous irritability toward those who speak of "generations." Interviewed in the *New Leader* (February 23, 1959), he delivered the following philippic: "Take Jack Kerouac and his *On The Road,* the tale's been told before, and better. There's little attention to style and no discipline. And this talk of a 'Beat Generation.' The whole subject of 'generations' seems to me to be a crashing bore. Some huckster picks up some idiotic and misleading classification, like the 'Lost' or the 'Beat,' and drums it into everybody's ears until you'd think they'd vomit. The odd thing is that they don't. All these pigeonholes relieve people of the effort to use their own minds. I say to hell with them." Several years earlier Dos Passos wrote a short essay taking issue with the eulogists and commentators who had responded to the death of Fitzgerald by labeling him a member of

"The Chronicles of Dos Passos" by Richard Chase. From *Commentary* (May 1961), pp. 395–400. Reprinted by permission of *Commentary* and Mrs. Frances W. Chase, Executrix of Estate of Richard V. Chase.

the "lost generation" and asserting that he had never been able to get beyond the attitudes of the disillusioned 1920's and had thus become increasingly irrelevant as a novelist. Dos Passos went on to praise Fitzgerald's novel *The Last Tycoon,* left unfinished at his death, for its quality of "detaching itself from its period while embodying its period." He thought that in this novel Fitzgerald had established for the first time "that unshakable moral attitude toward the world we live in and toward its temporary standards that is the basic essential of any powerful work of the imagination. A firmly anchored ethical standard is something that American writing has been struggling toward for half a century."

Clearly there is something personal in all this, and the truth is, of course, that Dos Passos himself has been customarily labeled a member of the defunct lost generation, though with a difference. The difference is that although he undertook immediately after World War I to live and to write about all the accredited experiences of the disillusioned yet romantic group that included Hemingway, E. E. Cummings, and Fitzgerald, he was able to speed along into the 1930's in high gear while the others faltered, halted, or backtracked. With sufficient prescience one might have predicted that this would be so on the evidence of Dos Passos' war novel *Three Soldiers* (1921). For despite its similarity to other works of the period, such as Hemingway's *The Sun Also Rises* and *A Farewell to Arms,* it differs from these by showing the author's strongly emerging interest in the social and political structure of modern civilization. The nature of the army bureaucracy behind the battle line fascinated Dos Passos as much as did the combat experience (of which the novel takes little notice), or even the aesthetic and moral yearnings, the love affairs, and the growing despair of the hero, although the private life and death of the hero are the novel's main focus. Thus, after the somewhat abortive but still remarkably interesting *Manhattan Transfer* (1925), full of transitions of attitude and experiments in form, he was able to embark on the three related novels which he published between 1930 and 1936 (*The 42nd Parallel, Nineteen Nineteen,* and *The Big Money*) and which he brought together under the title *U. S. A.* This impressive chronicle of American life from the turn of the century down to the eve of the depression is generally said to represent the culmination of Dos Passos' power as a novelist, beyond which none of his subsequent writings has been able to go, except chronologically.

But despite the fact that *U. S. A.* is worlds apart from the early novels of Hemingway and Fitzgerald, and differs in many ways from those of Dos Passos himself, this enormous work failed to liberate the author from the lost- generation category. As the years have gone on Dos Passos has become more and more the moralist, journalist, historian, and chronicler and has continued to be a novelist mostly by drawing repeatedly on the limited arsenal of techniques and literary devices which he experimented with in *Manhattan Transfer* and worked out fully in *U. S. A.* And it has become increasingly difficult not to think of Dos Passos, the significant novelist, as existing in the early works up to and including *U. S. A.,* and of these early works as something of a unit. Alfred Kazin's idea (see *On Native Grounds*) that *U. S. A.* was still a lost-generation novel with the single difference that the doomed hero was society itself, rather than the sensitive young man who usually figured in such novels, seems as true as it ever did.[1]

Yet this "single difference" has apparently been the crucial circumstance in Dos Passos' subsequent development or, since this is the point, lack of development. For one thing, it strikes me that Dos Passos' faculties of sympathy and imagination were damaged early in his career because, with all the machine-like efficiency of his mind, he annihilated the sensitive, suffering, aspiring young hero, a projection of himself, whom we meet in the earliest books. If Faulkner and Hemingway have shown more power of development and change in the long run than has Dos Passos it is in part because they did not annihilate their youthful selves but found new forms in which they could appear and new worlds in which they could live. But let me return to this a bit later.

Certainly Dos Passos' new novel, *Midcentury,* inspires one to observe *plus ça change,* etc. With modifications the author still relies on the external effects of immediacy and topicality which he achieved in *U. S. A.* by means of what he called the camera eye, the

1. [See pp. 101–19 of this volume.—Ed.]

newsreel, and the biography. In the new novel the biographies—
short impressionistic sketches interspersed among the passages of fiction in somewhat whimsical typographic arrangements—have a
measure of the old vividness, as in the portraits of John L. Lewis,
General MacArthur, Senator McClellan, Dave Beck, Walter Reu-
ther, and Mrs. Roosevelt (although in the latter biography Dos
Passos seems hardly able to restrain himself from telling some of
the famous improper jokes, so strong is his contempt for "the
rover"). There is less of the camera eye in this novel than one might
have hoped for, less, that is, of the personal, introspective reminis-
cence Dos Passos likes to cast, often with rather embarrassing results, into poetic form by breaking up the lines and using italics
(from these passages one sometimes gets the impression that Dos
Passos believes poetry can be produced by writing prose and then
crossing out the the's, a's and my's). The newsreels—pastiches of
headlines and brief topical quotations calculated to give one a
sense of the idiocy of the culture—are still effective.

But all this is only what meets the eye first. The novel proper consists of several interwoven stories—contrived fables, really—dealing
with various aspects of the labor movement, plus one calculated
apparently to show that businessmen too are human. Although Dos
Passos has written a good deal about the labor movement in earlier
novels, this is the first time he has made it his main subject, redeeming, thus, a promise of long standing. From one point of view *Mid-
century* is interesting by default, there being so little good fiction
devoted to what would seem to be a rich and significant subject.
There was no shortage of novels about labor in the 30's, but with
the exception of one or two, notably Robert Cantwell's *Land of
Plenty,* these novels were so simple-minded and so charged with an
apocalyptic but still tiresome ideology that they make dreary reading today. Sinclair Lewis never did get around to redeeming *his*
promise to write a labor novel revolving about a Eugene Debs-like
character. If he had, it would doubtless seem to us to be somewhat
shallow intellectually and superficial in its grasp of political realities.
Still, there is no doubt that it would have been sharp, satirical, and
amusing, and sometimes, coming up for air from Dos Passos' effi-

cient, relentless pages, one wishes one could turn to Lewis' unwritten book.

The "unshakable moral attitude" Dos Passos believes the novel must move toward is in *Midcentury,* and with a vengeance. The reader who (like myself) is ready to become just as disturbed as Dos Passos about corruption and all the ills and injustices of bigness in the modern labor movement, but who would also like to read a good novel on the subject, will feel let down by the author's willingness to forgo the requirements of good fiction in order to contrive his fables for didactic purposes—see the long stories or short novels about Terry Bryant and Frank Worthington. The lesson Dos Passos teaches is familiar to anyone who has followed his later career, but it may be news (probably good news) to many of the readers who are currently sending the book up the best-seller list that the author finds virtually nothing good in the labor movement since the heroic days of independence and intransigence exemplified by the IWW.

The best part of the book consists of the several sections devoted to the story of Blackie Bowman. In this story of an itinerant "working stiff"—an individualist and perpetual seeker for freedom who in his youth had become involved with the Wobblies and with bohemian intellectuals and artists and had participated in such causes as the great strike of the silk mills in Paterson, New Jersey (not to mention the absurd Madison Square Garden pageant that allegorized the strike)—Dos Passos is doing what in essence he has often done before, but he is still doing it well. Even so, as always, there is something a bit too self-conscious in Dos Passos' projection of himself as a working stiff. Once in a while in reading this novel you want to exclaim: Come off it, O solemn chronicler—son of Harvard, aesthete *manqué,* squire of country acres—what do you *really* know about working stiffs? But Dos Passos is not the first in this country's roster of patrician radical-reactionaries—that valuable species—to project himself incongruously.

Except in passing, I have not until now raised the matter of Dos Passos' reactionary political views as these have evolved in recent years, although I believe many people who undertook to say something about this author would have begun by talking about his views and pointing out the supposed damage they have done to his fiction. It has become a cliché of routine liberalism that when Dos Passos gave up his earlier liberal-radical convictions, supported Senator Taft for president, and began to write for the *National Review,* his powers of imagination failed, his capacity for human sympathy dwindled, and his view of life in general became narrow, bleak, humorless, and grim. I do not myself find this very persuasive. The limited imagination, the hard-boiled stance, the bleakness and grimness—all these can be seen in *U. S. A.*

In a sense, Dos Passos' views have not changed as much as would appear, a fact on which the author likes to insist. After his early "Marxism" and attraction to the Communist party, his disaffection from which is chronicled in *Adventures of a Young Man,* Dos Passos fell back on a temperamental, individualistic dissidence, which, in different contexts, may be as significantly practiced by a reactionary capitalist as by a revolutionary anarchist. A self-proclaimed "Jeffersonian," Dos Passos has preached ever since the New Deal that we must decline every gambit of organized political power. This may be quixotic as political theory, but it is morally sound and not likely in itself to damage the imagination of a novelist. In the light of Dos Passos' later career, one begins to see, by the way, that he has perhaps owed less to Marx and Veblen (who influenced him far more than Marx) than to John Dos Passos, Sr. The novelist's father was a brilliant man in his way, a lawyer and maverick Republican who wrote books on jurisprudence and related matters and whose views were a curious mixture of crusty reaction and democratic idealism.

Like his father, Dos Passos has the impulse of the pamphleteer, which is what he has increasingly become since *Manhattan Transfer.* His fictions are inspired less by imagination than by anger and zeal, and are alive, all too often, not with the thriving independent life of the characters who appear in them but with the egotism and assertiveness of the author. And this is true of *U. S. A.*, it seems to me, even though we remember with an impression of their vividness the main figures of that grandiose social pageant: Fenian McCreary, Janey Williams, J. Ward Moorehouse, Richard Savage, and the rest.

If Dos Passos' fictions are not quite able to possess our minds as fictions, it is partly because he has never found a language that we recognize as his. One cannot open a book by Hemingway or Faulkner without knowing immediately that one is in a unique world fashioned by the author's own idiom. Yet I'm not sure that if I were presented with a spot passage by Dos Passos I could tell who wrote it, unless one of the familiar external devices (the camera eye, etc.) were visible or unless I hit on one of his pormanteau words like the irksome one in the new novel: "dimshining." (No doubt "dimshining mist" is very poetical, but how does one get rid of the first impression that "dimshining" is a typographical scramble of "diminishing"?

Dos Passos' external devices are so obtrusive as to make us suspect that they are a mechanical attempt to establish a unique style and language not otherwise forthcoming. Clearly Dos Passos has *wanted* to discover a language which would be *internal*, in the sense of being an organic quality of his fiction, informing the whole with its tonality and structure. This quest for a language is suggested in the prologue to *U. S. A.* Here we have the familiar theme of the homeless young man on the road, and after a Whitmanesque catalogue of the places he has been to, the young man muses "it was the speech that clung to the ears, the link that tingled in the blood; U. S. A. . . . mostly U. S. A. is the speech of the people." This may remind us of other writers who are in the Whitman tradition: Thomas Wolfe— "Remembering speechlessly we seek the great forgotten language"— and William Carlos Williams—"What common language to unravel?" And it reminds us of Whitman himself, the Whitman of *Democratic Vistas,* who says that it is the duty of American writers to find a language which is at once a personal style and an archetypal expression of the culture. Lacking the thaumaturgic power to turn this difficult trick, Dos Passos has manufactured over the years a style that is energetic, efficient, and mostly anonymous.

Everyone speaks of Dos Passos' integrity and of his single-minded devotion to his work. These are admirable qualities, but the artistic implications of his particular kind of integrity are worth reflection.

In the essay on Fitzgerald, he wrote that "to attain the invention of any sound thing, no matter how trivial, demands the integrated effort of somebody's whole heart and whole intelligence." This sounds convincing, but we also read that "no durable piece of work, either addressed to the pulps or to the ages, has ever been accomplished by a double-minded man." Here we are brought up short. We think of the famous "doubleness" of Hawthorne, Melville, Mark Twain, and so many other important American writers, including Fitzgerald. We may even think of the persistent polarities of American culture itself, and we wonder whether Dos Passos has never perceived these facts (he whose most famous utterance is "allright we are two nations"!), or whether he has perceived them and decided that they are sources of weakness only, and never of strength—in which case he is at odds with almost everyone else who has been reflecting during the last two or three decades on the "double-mindedness" of our best writers.

But perhaps this is to take his words too seriously. It is hard to tell, because he does not make clear what opposing quantities are contained in the doubleness of which he speaks. He is ostensibly pointing out nothing more complicated than that Fitzgerald suffered as a man and writer because he tried to satisfy both Mammon and his own conscience and that these irreconcilable purposes left him with an agonizing "split personality." But out of Fitzgerald's case Dos Passos attempts to generalize on doubleness, and here is where the obscurity sets in. "The young American proposing to write a book," he says, "is faced by the world, the flesh and the devil on the one hand and on the other by the cramped schoolroom of the highbrows with its flyblown busts of the European great and its priggish sectarian attitudes. There's popular fiction and fortune's bright roulette wheel, and there are the erratic aspirations of the longhaired men and shorthaired women who, according to the folklore of the time, live on isms and Russian tea, and absinthe and small magazines of verse. Everybody who has put pen to paper during the last twenty years has been plagued by the difficulty of deciding whether he's to do 'good' writing that will satisfy his conscience or 'cheap' writing that will satisfy his pocketbook." Leaving aside one's impression that this rather fantastic picture of American culture comes from middlebrow folklore rather than direct observation, we are amazed to find that after the sarcastic remarks about highbrows, " 'good' writing" is being identified (so it would seem) both as what the highbrows demand and "what will satisfy" the writer's "conscience." Perhaps this is merely an example of careless or incompleted argument (I don't think the nervous quotes around "good" clear anything up). Or it may be just another example of the untenable position of the middlebrow polemist, with his routine attack on the highbrow and then his admission, conscious or not, of dependence on him.

If the polarities of Dos Passos' cultural dialectic are not very clear, there is no doubt that he is against them. "Doubleness" may have a variety of meanings, referring, for example, to an impulse toward Mammon and an impulse toward disinterested art, a genteel morality consorting uneasily with a demonic imagination, a sexual ambivalence, or simply the power (as Fitzgerald put it) "to hold two opposed ideas in the mind at the same time, and still retain the ability to function." In any case I would not suppose that a psychic doubleness is something to be pursued on purpose, even though it can obviously be a source of great strength. And there is of course much to be said for Dos Passos' ideal of "the integrated effort of somebody's whole heart and whole intelligence." Still, if psychological truth induces us to speak of the two Mark Twains, the two Fitzgeralds, etc., it also induces us to speak of the one Dos Passos.

What would have kept Dos Passos' mind freer, more accommodating, and more flexible? I have only a suggestion, based on the fact that *Manhattan Transfer* is my favorite among the author's books. In this work Jimmie Herf, the sensitive unhappy young man, who is rather obviously Dos Passos himself, is at the center of the action, as was John Andrews, the aspiring composer from Harvard, in *Three Soldiers*. In later works the Dos Passos figure is either moved into the periphery or rather violently transmogrified into the itinerant "working stiff" or political seeker. Thus the early books with their vital interplay between the young hero and society came to be replaced by books which lack the author's immediate, personal, and emotional sense of the happenings he describes as they bear upon his most cherished inner aspirations. The famous machine-like style, the angry intelligence, and the encyclopedic reportorial observation were won at too great an emotional cost (as is suggested by the novel of two years ago, *The Great Days,* evidently a book of more or less distant "spiritual" autobiography and one of Dos Passos' weakest works). By contrast to Dos Passos' unhappy annihilation of his youthful self, callow and overly sensitive as this self may have been, both Faulkner and Hemingway have transformed, without obliterating, their earlier selves into a series of later characters. Just as Quentin Compson of *The Sound and the Fury* lives on in the Gavin Stevens of Faulkner's later works, so Hemingway's Nick Adams (*In Our Time*) lives on in a character like Santiago in *The Old Man and the Sea.*

It can be said, to be sure, that Dos Passos' early self-portraits were not so interesting to begin with as were those of Faulkner and Hemingway. This is true, but his young heroes are still very much worth our attention. At the end of *Manhattan Transfer,* Jimmy Herf sets out on the road with three cents. He is in a mood of euphoria, his hero of the moment being a man in Philadelphia who was shot for wearing a straw hat too early in the spring. But Jimmie Herf is not being merely flip. It is not only the man with the straw hat that occupies his mind; he is genuinely in quest of selfhood and reality. Reality, which a novelist ought to be able to conceive of as plastic, fecund, emergent, and in motion among balances and tensions, had become for Dos Passos in *U. S. A.* a fixed idea: reality was a great, grim, menacing monolith against which all good things are broken. The quest for selfhood came to interest him no longer, because it seemed to be the preoccupation of the self-indulgent, romantic, highbrow decade of the 20's. But the trouble is that in the mind of every great novelist reality remains unfixed and the discovery and fulfillment of the self are a perpetual possibility.

Chronology of Important Dates

1896   John Dos Passos born in Chicago. His father was a lawyer, the son of a Portuguese immigrant; his mother's family came from Maryland and Virginia.

1916   Graduated *cum laude* from Harvard University having previously been educated at the Choate School. Went to Spain to study architecture.

1917   After his father's death, joined the Norton-Harjes Ambulance Unit, and served in Italy and France. "World War I then became my University."

1920   *One Man's Initiation: 1917*

1921   *Three Soldiers*

1921–22   With Near-East Relief in the Caucasus

1923   *Streets of Night*

1925   *Manhattan Transfer*

1926   Joined executive board of *New Masses*.

1927   *Facing the Chair* (A pamphlet written for the Sacco-Vanzetti Defense Committee). Worked with New Playwrights Theatre group.

1928   Six months' visit to Russia.

1930   *The 42nd Parallel*

1932   *1919*

1936   *The Big Money*

1937   Visited Spain during the Civil War. His friend José Robles Pazos executed by the Communist Loyalists.

1939   *Adventures of a Young Man*

1943   *Number One*

1947   Wife killed in automobile accident.

1949   *The Grand Design*. Remarried.

1951   *Chosen Country*

1954   *The Head and Heart of Thomas Jefferson*

1961   *Mid-Century*

1967   *The Best Times*

1970   Dies.

Notes on the Editor and Contributors

ANDREW HOOK is Senior Lecturer in English at the University of Aberdeen, Scotland, with special responsibility for the teaching of American literature. He has edited *Waverley* by Sir Walter Scott and (with Judith Hook) *Shirley* by Charlotte Brontë.

RICHARD CHASE (1914–1966), critic, scholar, and biographer. His books include *Herman Melville: A Critical Study, Emily Dickinson, Walt Whitman Reconsidered,* and *The American Novel and Its Tradition.*

MALCOLM COWLEY, critic and editor, is the author of several studies of modern American writing: *Exile's Return, After the Genteel Tradition, The Literary Situation.*

BLANCHE GELFANT, author of *The American City Novel,* is Professor of English, State University of New York, Upstate Medical Center, Syracuse.

GRANVILLE HICKS, author, editor, and critic. His books include *The Great Tradition, The Living Novel, Part of the Truth: An Autobiography.*

ALFRED KAZIN is the author of such notable works as *On Native Grounds, The Inmost Leaf,* and *Starting Out in the Thirties.*

F. R. LEAVIS is Honorary Visiting Professor of English at the University of York, England. His major critical works include *Revaluation, New Bearings in English Poetry, The Common Pursuit, The Great Tradition,* and *D. H. Lawrence: Novelist.*

E. D. LOWRY is Professor of English at Dunbarton College of Holy Cross, Washington, D. C.

CLAUDE-EDMONDE MAGNY, who died in 1966, was a distinguished French critic with a special interest in modern French and American fiction.

HERBERT MARSHALL MCLUHAN, Professor of English at the University of Toronto, has published several influential works on literature and communication such as *The Gutenberg Galaxy* and *Understanding Media.*

ARTHUR MIZENER is Professor of Humanities at Cornell University. His books include *The Far Side of Paradise* and *The Saddest Story: a Biography of Ford Madox Ford.*

WALTER B. RIDEOUT, Professor of American Literature, University of Wisconsin, has edited *Letters of Sherwood Anderson.*

JEAN-PAUL SARTRE is a distinguished French novelist, playwright, critic and existentialist philosopher.

LIONEL TRILLING is Professor of Literature at Columbia University. His many books include *Matthew Arnold, The Liberal Imagination, The Opposing Self, Sincerity and Authenticity.*

JOHN WILLIAM WARD is Professor of History at Amherst College. He has published *Andrew Jackson, Symbol for an Age* and *The Nature and Tendency of Free Institutions.*

T. K. WHIPPLE is the author of *Spokesmen: Modern Writers and American Life.*

EDMUND WILSON (1895–1972), one of America's distinguished men of letters. Author of some thirty books.

Selected Bibliography

No biography of Dos Passos has yet appeared, and none of his correspondence has been published.

BOOKS ON DOS PASSOS

Astre, Georges-Albert. *Thèmes et structures dans l'oeuvre de John Dos Passos.* Paris: Minard, 1956, 1958, p. 58.

Belkind, Allen, ed., *Dos Passos, the Critics, and the Writer's Intention.* Carbondale and Edwardsville: Southern Illinois University Press, 1971.

Brantley, John D. *The Fiction of John Dos Passos,* Studies in American Literature, Vol. 16. The Hague: Mouton, 1968.

Wrenn, John H. *John Dos Passos.* New Haven: Twayne, 1961.

SECTIONS OF BOOKS

Aaron, Daniel. "The Adventures of John Dos Passos." In *Writers on the Left,* New York: Harcourt, Brace, 1961.

Aldridge, John W. "Dos Passos: The Energy of Despair." In *After the Lost Generation.* New York: McGraw-Hill, 1951.

Beach, Joseph Warren. *American Fiction: 1920–1940.* New York: Macmillan, 1941. Pp. 25–66.

Blake, N. M. "The Rebels." In *Novelists' America: Fiction as History, 1910–1940.* Syracuse, N.Y.: Syracuse University Press, 1969.

Frohock, W. M. "John Dos Passos: Of Time and Frustration." In *The Novel of Violence in America.* Dallas: Southern Methodist University Press, 1957.

Geismar, Maxwell. "John Dos Passos: Conversion of a Hero." In *Writers in Crisis.* Boston: Houghton-Mifflin, 1942.

185

Gurko, Leo. "John Dos Passos' 'U.S.A.': A 1930's Spectacular." In *Proletarian Writers of the Thirties,* ed. David Madden. Carbondale and Edwardsville: Southern Illinois University Press, 1968.

Lee, Brian. "History and John Dos Passos." In *The American Novel and the Nineteen Twenties,* ed. M. Bradbury and D. Palmer. London: Edwin Arnold, 1971.

Lydenberg, John. "Dos Passos' *U.S.A.*: The Words of the Hollow Men." In *Essays on Determinism in American Literature,* ed. S. J. Krause. Kent, Ohio: Kent State University Press, 1964.

Millgate, Michael. "John Dos Passos." In *American Social Fiction.* New York: Barnes and Noble, 1964.

Mizener, Arthur. "The Big Money." In *Twelve Great American Novels.* New York: New American Library, 1967.

Thorp, Willard. *American Writing in the Twentieth Century.* Cambridge, Mass.: Harvard University Press, 1963. Pp. 136–42.

ARTICLES

Beach, Joseph Warren. "Dos Passos: 1947." *Sewanee Review,* 55 (1947).

Gelfant, Blanche H. "The Search for Identity in the Novels of John Dos Passos." *PMLA,* 76 (1961).

Goldman, Arnold. "Dos Passos and His *U.S.A.*" *New Literary History,* 1 (1970).

Lowry, E. D. "The Lively Art of *Manhattan Transfer.*" *PMLA,* 84 (1969).

Sanders, David. " 'Lies' and the System: Enduring Themes from Dos Passos' Early Novels." *South Atlantic Quarterly,* 65 (1966).

Schwartz, Delmore. "John Dos Passos and the Whole Truth." *Southern Review,* 4 (1938).

Stoltzfus, Ben. "John Dos Passos and the French." *Comparative Literature,* 15 (1963).